WEIGHT ROOM WISDOM

RON MCKEEFERY

Dedication

To the four humans I hope to inspire the most, strive each day to make it better than the last and work tirelessly to leave this world better than you found it. Love you more than you will ever know Tyler, Ava, Maya and James.

#TeamMcKeefery

TABLE OF CONTENTS

Forward

G. K. Chesterton writes that everyone loves two things: people and stories. Anybody who aspires to be a teacher needs to learn this lesson quickly. In teaching, we have a long tradition of basing education methods on three simple elements: stories, pictures and questions. The great teachers are invariably the great storytellers. Although students may never become aware that they are learning, teachers that engage their students' imaginations demonstrate the gift of their craft.

When Jesus explained the Kingdom of God to his audiences, used parables of mustard seeds, great pearls, and buried treasure. When asked about forgiveness, he told a story about two brothers and another of a servant who owed money.

My old lifting coach, Dick Notmeyer, ran a paper route for the San Francisco Chronicle. Each morning, he would get up around 3 am and make his rounds. He would get home close to noon and nap for a few hours before opening his gym. The Pacifica Barbell Club was a back room of a garage. It had a platform for lifting, a few racks, a bench and a foundry of weights. Each afternoon, Dick would teach all comers how to lift in the Olympic style. Of course, he charged dues. As a student, I paid the hefty sum of a quarter per week. That's all he charged.

When I met Dick, we were in the midst of a family crisis. My father had lost his license due to a second DUI as I finished high school. His career was in jeopardy, and the company he worked for was about to close. My choices were limited: the military or athletics. After failing to develop as a slow, skinny defensive back, I rolled the dice on the discus. And then I met Dick.

Between sets in the weight room, Dick would often tell stories about other lifters. He often added: "Oh, he was a skinny guy like you, but then we got him." His stories showed me a path. Sometimes, he talked about guys who didn't make it, but always noted that they failed because of dope, booze, or other gym sins. Every problem seemed to lead to a story. And with each story, the road became clearer: don't miss workouts, eat a big breakfast, train hard and take your time. After two years of training five days each week in Dick's backroom, I showed him a letter from Utah State. I'd earned a scholarship.

We all need people like Dick Notmeyer: someone to tell us the stories. Someone to point us on the way. As I always remind teachers and coaches, it's not my story. It's ours. And it needs to be told.

Storytelling
Dan John
Coach and Author - DanJohn.net

Introduction

My junior year in college was one of the toughest years of my life. In retrospect, coming off of a 1-9 season probably shouldn't have warranted such intensity. But in the moment, nothing else mattered. As I sat in our stretch lines, staring at our new Head Football Coach that first winter workout, I was cautiously optimistic. Were we going to be able to get it turned around? Was our 26-year-old Head Football Coach ready for the challenge? Was I ready to lead the team as a senior?

Just as we were about to finish stretch, Coach Creighton started in on a story about John Goddard, about whom a Life Magazine article was published in 1972. At age 15, John Goddard had written down 127 "Life Purposes" for his future. These were not your typical goals, but rather included things like:

• Explore rivers Nile, Amazon, Congo, Colorado, Yangtze, Niger, Orinoco, and Rio Coco.

• Climb mountains Everest, Aconcagua, McKinley, Huascaran, Kilimanjaro, Arafat, Kenya, Cook, Popocatépetl, Matterhorn, Rainier, Fuji, Vesuvius, Bromo, Grand Tetons, Baldy, and Ayers Rock.

• For adventure, achievement and cultural development, he concluded his list with 55 purposes, including: become an Eagle Scout, dive in a submarine, land on and take off from an aircraft carrier, ride an elephant (and a camel and an ostrich and a bronco), dive to 40 feet (holding breath for two and a half minutes underwater), catch a 10 lb. lobster and a 10" abalone, play the flute and the violin, type 50 words per minute, make a parachute jump, learn water skiing and regular skiing, go on a church mission, study native medicines (bring back useful ones), bag camera trophies of elephant (and lion, rhino, cheetah, cape buffalo, and whale), learn fencing and jiu-jitsu, teach a college course, watch a cremation ceremony in Bali, explore the sea depths, build a telescope, write a book, publish an article in National Geographic, high jump 5 feet, broad jump 15 feet, weigh 175 lbs., perform 200 sit-ups and 20 pull-ups in one session, learn French (and Spanish and Arabic), visit the birthplaces of Grandfather Sorenson in Denmark and Grandfather Goddard in England, ship aboard a freighter as a seaman, read the Bible from cover to cover, read the works of Shakespeare (and Plato, Aristotle, Dickens, Thoreau, Rousseau, Hemingway, Twain, Burroughs, Talmage and Tolstoy), etc.

I don't know about you, but at 42 years of age, I can't even pronounce some of those names, much less think to set them as "Life Purposes" at age 15. That night in my dorm room, I sat down and wrote my own list. I would be embarrassed to share it after relaying some of John's, but the point is that hearing his story compelled me to take action of my own.

I didn't realize it at the time, but Coach Creighton used the most powerful tool in the "Coach Toolbox" to drive home his message: storytelling. I wouldn't learn that until I stood in front of my own teams, searching for a way to keep their attention as I passed along messages of inspiration. Fortunately for me, I had the benefit of learning under Coach Creighton for a year as a player and another as a coach, so storytelling came fairly easily. However, I quickly realized that those who included stories in their messages tended to be the most successful coaches. I also realized that those who didn't often dried up in the profession.

Ask any coach why they got into the field of strength and conditioning. Nine out of ten will say they wanted to make an impact on young people. There are many ways that strength coaches do just that. General counseling, goal setting/accountability, and elite performance coaching are just a few of the common opportunities our work affords us to provide a positive influence on the lives of those we train. That said, I believe that the 5 minutes before and after a lift, when you get to talk with your players about being a better human, make as much of an impact as anything you will do as a strength and conditioning coach.

An average of three workouts per week per year for four years is over 600 workouts. That means at least 1,200 opportunities to help prepare your players for the field, and more importantly for the game of life. I love these moments! To me, they are the most precious gift we are given as coaches, and a blessing we must earn by constantly preparing different ways to deliver those life-empowering messages. As strength and conditioning coaches, we did not take classes in motivation, leadership, or motivational speaking. They may have been discussed in our Program Design and Physiology classes, but the skill is something that must be organically developed.

One of the best ways I have found to do this is to learn from the greats in our profession. At this point in my career, there is not a whole lot that I haven't seen when it comes to sets and reps, but there is not a coach I have watched work that I haven't learned a new way of delivering messages from. I have often said that if we all lived on the same street, we would BBQ every night. Unfortunately, we only get a few opportunities to come together each year, and we rarely get to watch each other work. That is why I wanted to put together Weight Room Wisdom.

Inspired by the old Chicken Soup for the Soul books, I have reached out to some of the very best in our profession to share with you the stories they use to inspire their athletes and coaches. The following stories are a collection of metaphorical, experiential and personal messages that some of the giants of our field are using on a daily basis to make better humans. Better humans make better players and coaches, and more importantly, they help contribute to a better world.

My hope for you is that one of these stories (or one that they inspire you to share) has the same impact on your athletes or coaches that the story of John Goddard had on me. That year, hearing his story inspired me to set both season goals and life goals. We went from 1-9 my junior year to 9-2 and the first Playoff appearance for Ottawa University in a number of years. More importantly, the list of goals I wrote in my dorm room that night has been transferred many times, but now lives as an Evernote document on my iPhone.

1

The Floor Sweeper
and the Window Washer

Mike Boyle

Mike Boyle Strength & Conditioning

We always hear coaches say things like "know your role" and "do your job." I think in college it's particularly tough for young men and women who have always been stars to accept lesser roles or ones they don't feel suited for.

Most every year, players will approach me who are unhappy with their roles. They say, "If only coach would realize that I'm better at [fill in the blank]." And I always tell them the same story. It goes like this:

Imagine a coach came to me and said, "Mike, I need a great floor sweeper. I know it's not a great job, but it's a place to start."

I respond with, "But coach, I'm a really great window washer."

The coach says, "That's great Mike, but I don't need a window washer this year. I need a great floor sweeper."

Now, imagine that I ignore the coach and every day when he comes to check on me, I'm washing the windows. Coach walks in and I say, "Coach, how do the windows look?"

Coach gets a little aggravated, looks down at the dirty floor and says, "Didn't you hear what I said about floor sweeping?"

After a few weeks, the coach comes in and fires me because I can't follow directions and don't understand my job. I think to myself, "But I'm a great window washer. Doesn't he see that?"

The point is, if the coach wants a floor sweeper, sweep the floors. And sweep them well. It doesn't matter what you think your job should be. It matters that you're doing what he expects of you. If the coach walks in and every day you're trying to do someone else's job, you will get "fired." Keep your head down, trust the process, and focus on becoming the best floor sweeper that coach has ever seen.

Athlete Huddle

When was the last time you were asked to "sweep the floors?" What did you learn from that experience?

Coach Huddle

What about when you've been sweeping the floors for a while and nobody seems to be noticing? What then? What is the goal?

2

The Prisoner's Dilemma

Brett Bartholomew

Strength Coach, Author Founder-Art of Coaching

The "Prisoner's Dilemma" is a famous example of a situation studied within the realm of game theory that elucidates reasons as to why two seemingly "rational" individuals may not choose to collaborate or cooperate. Specifically, the example lays out a scenario in which two criminals are captured by the police. The police believe that the two suspects are responsible for a murder, but don't have the necessary evidence to prove it in a court of law.

The prisoners are put in separate cells with no way of communicating or getting on the same page about their alibis.

The dilemma? If neither prisoner confesses, both will be convicted of a lesser offense and sentenced to a year in prison. If both confess to murder, both will be sentenced to five years. If, however, one prisoner confesses while the other does not, the prisoner who confesses will be granted immunity while the prisoner who does not will go to jail for 20 years. What should each prisoner do?

The example here highlights an issue that many coaches face internally, both with their staff and their athletes. The "dilemma" within our domain is the consequences of closed off or poor communication that often occurs due to ego, bias, insecurities, etc. These are all staples of human nature (no matter how educated or composed an individual may be) and, not only end up hampering, but also actively corroding the collaborative environments that are necessary when trying to accomplish a common end goal.

Coaches and athletes alike will, at times, pound their chests, stand their ground, and find ways for their concessions and agendas to be met. In complex social environments like these, it's best to hold your tongue, observe, and reflect, as opposed to trying to assert dominance or save your own skin. Remember, competition at the highest levels, by default, necessitates collaboration.

Athlete Huddle

Regardless of whether you compete in a team or individual sport, how did you feel when you knew, in order to get better, you had to "let go" and relinquish control to a process you didn't fully understand? What drove those emotions?

Coach Huddle

Think of a time when you were disrespected or met with resistance. Did you respond or react? In your mind, what are the hallmark differences between the two?

3

The Lion Tamer

Ron McKeefery

Vice President of Performance & Education - PLAE

One of my favorite memories from growing up is going to the circus. The one act that I remember most vividly was that of the lion tamer. I can see him now, entering the cage with his whip, a stool, and a few treats. There opposite him sits the king of beasts, three times his size. Now, you'd think that whip is his best defense, but it's not. The unlikely hero is the stool, not because it's threatening. No. It's confusing.

The lion seeks to lock in on its prey. But it can't. That floating stool, with its four legs, is more than the animal can process. Paralyzed, it sits, watching the tamer's antics, unable to move a muscle. The lion is not stupid. It knows it's bigger than the man. It knows this is a game it can easily win. But those four legs hypnotically keep it in a state of anticipation. It can't take action until its target is locked, and as long as the stool keeps moving, the lion waits on a razor's edge, just about ready to spring, just about ready to commit, and yet motionless.

Unfortunately, the same syndrome can overtake us when we try to focus on too many challenges at once. We become so over-stimulated, so overwhelmed, that we can't address any of them. We can't take action. We're paralyzed. Like the lion, we're not necessarily doubtful of our abilities to address a given situation. It's more like we're waiting. When certain

11

conditions are met, when certain pieces fall into place, when the dust settles – that's when we'll pounce. The problem is, dust rarely settles. The stool continues to bob, and if we allow our inertia to take over, we can easily camp out on that razor's edge, telling ourselves we're waiting for the opportune moment, completely oblivious to the fact that we're wasting valuable time.

Eat that lion tamer.

Athlete Huddle

What pieces are you waiting for to take the next step on your journey? Have you identified them?

Coach Huddle

Are you willing to be imperfect for the sake of serving your athletes?

4

Small and Personal

Kelly Starrett

Co-Founder-Mobility Wod/The Ready State

As coaches, we occasionally encounter situations in which our athletes face higher stakes than they've ever known before. The prospect of vying for a gold medal can cause a lot of anxiety for someone who's never ventured beyond a national competition (which might seem downright cozy in comparison). When these moments present themselves, we focus on keeping things small and personal. Here's an example.

Two hours before the Women's Olympic Rowing Final in the 2008 Beijing Games, one of our athletes (we'll call her E.) was having a moment. Early in her rowing career, and already a two-time National Champion, she'd worked her way onto the Olympic boat by grit and tenacity, outworking and outracing more seasoned athletes. She was the least experienced woman in the group. In that moment, E. couldn't contextualize her freakish talent and work ethic (she would go on to become one of the USA's best rowers ever). So we made the moment as granular and as mundane as possible.

We started by giving her competition a face. We had E. identify the athlete who was rowing in the same position as she was in the boat most likely to challenge them. That gave her a personal anchor. She didn't have to win a gold medal anymore; she just had to out-row one other person. We took it a step further. We asked E. to imagine a world in which that other athlete had defeated her by investing more effort into the race. We asked E. if she thought her competition had done a better job of recovering, sleeping, and even eating than she had.

Earlier in training, we had developed a competition strategy for E. when she had time trial testing on the erg. Because she had such a freakish capacity to suffer when it mattered, E. would set up her erg right next to her biggest threat. There would always be a moment when the athlete next to E. would break, and in that moment, E. would plan to increase her pace, thereby proving that she hadn't even reached her max effort. It was a brutal tactic, but it had landed her in the Olympic boat.

Now the moment had come, and E. needed a tactic to calm her nerves. Once she'd identified the girl she was rowing against, she "set up her erg" nearby. When confronted with the actual person, her clothes, hair, and all the other details, E. realized there was no way that single athlete could match her in the middle of the race, when the pain would be most intense. The Olympics was now just about a competition between two people, and E. wouldn't be outworked by anyone.

They won by nearly open water.

Athlete Huddle

How do you mentally prepare for your biggest moments in competition. What have you found to be your most effective tactics?

Coach Huddle

What do your athletes require most in a coach when the stakes of competition get super high? How can you meet those needs?

5

You Get What You Give

Lachlan Wilmot

Head of Athletic Performance/Co-Owner - Parramatta Eels NRL Club/Athletes Authority

Afarmer and a baker traded goods with one another. The farmer would bring a pound of butter, and the baker would offer a pound of bread in return. Their weekly arrangement lasted for years.

One day, after he left the farm, the baker began to suspect his friend of cheating. So to see if he was given the proper amount, he weighed the butter. Less than a pound.

Furious, the baker dragged the farmer into court and explained his grievance to the judge.

When he was finished, the judge turned to the farmer and asked why he hadn't delivered a full pound of butter to the baker. The farmer responded, "Your honor, I'm a simple man living a simple life. I don't use modern measuring methods. All I have is a scale."

"Then how do you measure your butter?" the judge inquired.

The farmer replied, "Every week, when the baker arrives to trade, I place his bread on my scale and give him back the same weight in butter. If anyone's to blame, it's him!"

Too often we focus on what we're getting instead of what we're giving. But there's no shortcut to success. And in the end, we determine by our own actions the kinds of people we become. Don't cheat yourself. Put the work in. And when it pays off, rest in the undeniable truth that you only get out of something what you put into it.

Athlete Huddle

You get what you give. What are you giving? How do you think it will affect your performance come game day?

Coach Huddle

Do you think your athletes can tell when you're not giving your all? What are you doing to ensure you get the most out of each session? Which strategies do you employ to push yourself toward improvement?

6

The Carpenter

Scott Sinclair

Director of Football Strength & Conditioning - University of Georgia

An elderly carpenter informed his employer that he was retiring. His work tired him out, and he wanted to spend more time with his wife and children. He'd miss the paycheck, but he'd get by.

His employer of course understood but was sorry to see such a hard-working, skillful craftsman go. As the carpenter was leaving, his boss called to him and asked a question. "Will you build just one more house before you leave? As a personal favor to me?" The carpenter reluctantly agreed.

The next day, he set to work on his last house. He worked diligently, but it soon became apparent that his heart was no longer in his work. He resorted to shoddy workmanship and began using inferior materials. All he could think about was finishing and going home for good. What an unfortunate way to end an exceptional career.

When the house was complete, the boss came to inspect the carpenter's work. After briefly examining it, he reaching into his pocket with a smile and handed the carpenter a shiny new key. "This house is yours," he said. "Please consider it a gift from me." The carpenter took the key, speechless, not knowing how to respond. What a shame. If he'd only known he was building his own house, he would have done so much more carefully.

We build our lives a day at a time, often putting less than our best into the work. In the end, we realize (perhaps with a shock) that we have to live in the houses we've built. If we could go back and do it over, what would we do differently? We have to choose daily what kind of houses we're building. Each moment matters, because the work we do today affects the life we live tomorrow.

Athlete Huddle

What kind of house are you building?

Coach Huddle

If every moment matters, how could you improve your program? How could you set an example for your athletes of building a house to be proud of?

7

Marshmallows

Nick Grantham

Performance Enhancement Specialist - NickGrantham.com

In the 1960s, researchers at Stanford University conducted a series of experiments to demonstrate whether children chose to delay gratification for greater rewards. After completing a simple task, each child was offered either a single marshmallow immediately or two marshmallows after a brief delay. Not surprisingly, those who elected to wait for two marshmallows demonstrated higher degrees of success in other areas of life than the kids who stuffed their faces straight away.

How is this relevant to sport? Well, you could say that both athletes and coaches encounter marshmallows every day. Quick fixes sound good. They promise easy gains in exchange for minimal effort. But the truth is and always has been that healthy, enduring progress requires work and time. That's why we must understand and respect the laws of delayed gratification if we are to achieve our career goals and enjoy long term success.

It's harder now than ever before. We live in a time and place that offers anything we want almost instantly. A quick Google search provides instant answers. We can stream music. We can procure instant credit online. If we want something, we can get it almost immediately! But none of that changes the fact that training and the adaptations we are chasing take time. You can't lift once and expect to be stronger. You can't train for a couple of weeks and expect to be a first-round pick. You can't eat clean for a few days and expect rippling abs.

If you want lasting success, you need to put the work in today, knowing that you may not see the rewards until much later. Discipline promises outcomes that nothing else can offer.

Athlete Huddle:

Are you ready to work hard, even though you may see results until later?

Coach Huddle:

What is your response when you see a marshmallow? Can you think of a time you jumped at a quick fix only to be disappointed?

8

Training for Life Through Adversity in Sports

Matt Balis

Director of Football Performance - Notre Dame

The game of football is just like life. When adversity hits and you feel like you can't continue on or that all your hard work isn't paying off, remember that the lessons you learn here will apply to the rest of your life.

In Rocky 6, Rocky's son is questioning life, saying how unfair it is. Rocky says to him, "It's not about how hard you hit, but how hard you can get hit and keep moving forward. It's about how much you can take and not give in."

Rocky is explaining to him that life isn't fair for any of us. The people that make it in life and achieve their goals are the ones who can continue to chase their dreams and goals despite the setbacks and challenges they face. Our society needs men who understand this principle and will not give in when adversity hits. As husbands and fathers, we can't be passive and refuse to accept responsibility for our families. We must lead them courageously. There is nothing more important than leading your family the right way. Our children need male role models who will lead them with courage against adversity and who don't give in to the temptations of life.

During your time here playing football, you will be challenged in many ways. You will get injured, be sore, have academic responsibilities to juggle. You may not get the playing time you deserve. You will have social pressures that come with being 18-24 years old. This is a great opportunity to learn how to deal with all of those challenges in a positive way: by leaning on your teammates and the positive role models in your life.

At the conclusion of your college football experience, you will be stronger (mentally and physically) than you could have ever imagined. However, it will be up to you to use these experiences when approaching your future life challenges.

Athlete Huddle

What's an example of a time you faced adversity and continued to press on?

Coach Huddle:

What example are you setting for the young men who look up to you?

9

Make the Rep or Die

Zach Even Esh

Founder - Underground Strength Gym

Guys, do you ever start warming up for a wrestling match or look at your opponent across the mat and think, I don't know if I can beat this guy. You know the moment you start thinking like that, it's over. It's done.

The same truth applies when you are about to make a big lift. In fact, even during warm-up sets, when you approach that bar, you have to be ready to do or die. You can't walk up to that bar unsure. Maybe I get it, maybe I don't. No, that never works.

There's a story of an old powerlifter who was about to squat 850 or 900 pounds, and his whole crew of training partners was there, trying to get him psyched up. They were cheering and carrying on, doing whatever they could think of to get him going. Then the lifter stopped as he approached the bar and started screaming. "Hey! Everyone get the hell out of this gym! Get out right now!"

His training partners were like, "Dude you can't do this! You need a spotter."

But the lifter responds, "No, I will make this rep or die. I will die under this barbell if I don't I don't make this rep. Get the hell out of here."

He kicks everyone out, locks the door, gets under the bar does the rep. Then he lets everyone back in. Guys, when the resistance hits you on that barbell, don't give up. Don't dump the bar. You make the rep or die. You carry that attitude with you when you wrestle, and you carry that attitude with you everywhere else you go.

Make the rep or die.

Athlete Huddle:

What difference would it make if you knew you couldn't fail? Does your mind get in the way of your success?

Coach Huddle:

How can you stimulate this mindset in your athletes?

10

Do You Know the Magic Number

Aaron Ausmus

West Region Sales - Sorinex

The magic number is simply the number of reps in any strength training session. Obviously, this magic number differs from day to day. My goal is to emphasize the power and importance of the rep. Each day, after the pre-lift warm up, I gather the athletes up, go over the plan, emphasize the important cues for each movement, and then talk about the magic number. This magic number is the number of reps, but how the reps are executed is what makes them magic.

For example, on a given day we might have 5 exercises. Each exercise has 4 sets, and each set has 5 reps. The magic number is 100. Each athlete has 100 opportunities to make our plan become a magic plan. What will their number be today? 83/100, 92/100, or 100/100? One subpar rep in each set in this example will sum up to 80 reps done correctly and 20 reps that had poor or questionable execution. Basically, the athlete trained at 80 percent capacity of the plan. One bad rep per set doesn't sound that serious until you put it into a big picture scenario.

80 percent success in a football season is approximately 9 wins, 3 losses. Athletes start off any season with talks and ambitions of going undefeated, winning it all, and how hard they are going to train. Addressing the magic number and talking about it consistently creates a forced awareness of the quality of each rep for the athlete. At the end of sessions,

our coaching staff discusses with our athletes what they honestly thought their magic number was that day. Sometimes, their reality and the coaches' observations are different. If so, then the coach has the opportunity to give the athlete honest feedback.

Overall, since implementing this technique, passion and focus have picked up in the weight room. I have always said that the quality of each training session starts with the first rep executed.

Athlete Huddle

What's more important to you, the number of reps or the quality of reps? Why?

Coach Huddle:

How are you emphasizing the importance of every rep?

11

Carrots, Eggs and Coffee Beans

Adam Feit

Coordinator of Physical and Mental Performance - Springfield College

A young man went to his father and complained about how his life was too hard. He didn't know how he was going to make it. He wanted to give up. He was tired of fighting and struggling. He wanted to throw the towel in once and for all. It seemed that as he solved one problem, a new one arose.

His father took him to the kitchen, where he filled three pots with water and placed them on heat. Soon the pots came to a boil. In the first, he placed carrots. In the second, he placed eggs. In the third, he placed ground coffee. He let them sit and boil without saying a word. In about twenty minutes, he turned off the burners. He grabbed the carrots out and placed them in a bowl. He pulled the eggs out and placed them in a bowl. Then he ladled the coffee out into a bowl. Turning to his son, he asked, "What do you see?"

"Carrots, eggs, and coffee," the young man replied. The father brought him closer and asked him to feel the carrots. He did and noted that they were soft. Then his father asked him to take an egg and break it. After removing the shell, he observed the hard-boiled egg. Finally, he sipped the coffee. It tasted good. He smiled.

"What does it mean, Dad?" His father explained that each of these objects had faced the same adversity: boiling water. But each had reacted differently. The carrot went in strong, hard and unrelenting. However, it softened in the water and became weak. The egg had been fragile. But, after being boiled, its inside became hard! The ground coffee beans were unique, however. While in the boiling water, they had changed the water.

"Which are you? When adversity knocks on your door, how do you respond? Are you a carrot, an egg, or a coffee bean?"

Athlete Huddle:

When did adversity knock on your door? How did you respond?

Coach Huddle:

What does adversity teach? What have you learned from struggling?

12

Starving Baker

Donnell Boucher

Assistant Athletic Director: Strength & Conditioning - The Citadel

Adapted from Habitudes by Tim Elmore:

Imagine a brand new bakery opens on your block. It's the talk of the town. People line up to get a taste of the baker's exclusive treats. You go in and watch the baker in amazement. He's a one-man show. Not only is he a genius baker. He cleans, rings, greets and serves his customers.

The buzz continues and the crowd grows. You visit regularly and begin to notice something after three short months. The baker doesn't have enough help, but persists in trying to do it all. He prides himself in all areas of his business and can't let any responsibility go. He hustles so hard, sometimes skipping meals, and even spends all night at work. His hustle is feeding the customers, but starving himself. If this continues, his exhaustion will turn into burnout and ultimately a failed business.

Leaders can place so much focus on feeding others that they forget to feed themselves. You can't do your best work if you're starving - physically, mentally, or emotionally. We must nourish ourselves if we plan to stay effective. An empty cup cannot pour into another.

Athlete Huddle

What are you doing to invest in your personal well being beyond physical training?

Coach Huddle

What are strategies you can use to keep your cup full now and in the future?

14

Earn the Jersey

Ken Mannie

Head Strength & Conditioning Coach - Michigan State University

I talk a lot about the power of brotherhood. Proverbs calls it iron sharpening iron. Ancient Spartan warriors understood this concept. So does the United States Marine Corps. I routinely point to these examples when explaining our "earn the jersey" mentality.

Herodotus, an ancient Greek historian, said that when Spartan warriors fought individually, they were as good as any. But when they fought as a group, they were the greatest soldiers in the world. From early in their youth, Spartan boys were taught that their greatest strength as warriors was the soldier standing beside them. The Spartan phalanx was a meticulously crafted formation with the objective of delivering a powerful, impenetrable impact on the battlefield. With their long spears, glistening bronze shields, and ferocious, crested helmets, the Spartan phalanx sent many foes into immediate retreat at first sight. The Spartan shield was designed to protect the left half of the bearer, as well as the right half of the warrior to his side. If you caused any gap in the phalanx, you put your brothers in arms at risk. If you returned from battle without your helmet, you were fined. If you came back without your shield, you were executed. Hence the famous Spartan battle cry, proclaimed by wives and mothers as their soldiers departed for battle, "Come back with your shield or on it!"

Spartan principles apply to our teams, as well. What one player does affects the entire team. We urge our athletes to protect their reputations, to be careful in choosing what they put their names on. As Michigan Spartans, their names are always accompanied by those of their teammates. We are one.

Another great example is that of the 300 Spartans at Thermopylae. That small army, augmented by its allies, was able to hold off the massive Persian invasion for several days, due to its strategic use of the terrain and superior fighting skills. Those Spartans made history not just with swords, but with belief in each other, courage, heart, and relentless spirit. In the same way, we ask our athletes to charge into every challenge with a "never say die" mindset. Go in fast, go in strong, and go in with your brothers.

The Marine Corps Manifesto, which is clearly posted in its entirety on our weight room wall, has a profound message. It says, "You will be measured not by how much you have, but by how much of yourself you are willing to give." We want to replicate that sentiment in our mental, physical, and emotional development as Spartans. In essence, Spartans "earn their jerseys" because being a part of this group is an honor.

Athlete Huddle

What do you take pride   How important is your name to you? Your reputation?

Coach Huddle:

does it mean to you be part of a brotherhood, to defend those nding by your side as you would defend yourself?

15

The Parable of the Businessman and the Fisherman

Scott Caulfield

Head Strength & Conditioning Coach - NSCA Headquarters

A successful businessman on vacation was at the pier of a small coastal village when a small boat with just one fisherman docked. Inside the small boat were several large fish. The businessman complimented the fisherman on the quality of his haul and asked how long it had taken to catch them.

The fisherman proudly replied, "Every morning, I go out in my boat for 30 minutes to fish. I'm the best fisherman in the village."

The businessman probed. "If you're the best, why don't you stay out longer and catch more fish? What do you do the rest of the day?"

The fisherman replied, "I sleep late, fish a little, play with my children, spend quality time with my wife, and every evening we stroll into the village to drink wine and play guitar with our friends. I have a full and happy life."

The businessman scoffed, "I am a successful CEO and have a talent for recognizing business opportunities. I can help you become more successful. You should spend more time fishing and, with the proceeds, buy a bigger boat. With the proceeds from the bigger boat, you could buy several boats. Eventually, you would have a fleet of fishing boats with many fishermen. Instead of selling your catch to just your friends, you can scale and sell fish to thousands. You could leave this small coastal village and move to the big city where you can oversee your growing empire."

The fisherman asked, "But how long will this all take?"

"About 15-20 years."

"But then what?"

The businessman laughed and said, "That's the best part. When the time is right, you would sell your company stock to the public and become very rich. You would make millions!"

"Millions. Then what?" said the fisherman.

"Then you would retire. You'd move to a small coastal fishing village where you would sleep late, fish a little, play with your kids, spend time with your wife, stroll to the village in the evenings where you could sip wine and play your guitar with your friends."

Athlete Huddle

What would you do if you were the fisherman? Are you living in the moment or spending your time thinking about the future? How do you think living in the moment and being grateful for what you have can help you reach your goals?

Coach Huddle

Are you aware of what you have that is special in your life? Do you worry about things that are outside of your control? Everyone has choices. You can be the fisherman or the businessman. Which one do you want to be?

16

Finish the Race

Aaron Wellman

NCAA & NFL Performance Coach - New York Giants

One of the great moments in Olympic history took place on October 20, 1968, the final day of the Mexico City Games. Traditionally, the last event to be held was the men's marathon. 75 runners began their grueling, high-altitude trek at 3:00 pm, but the heroic moment to which I refer didn't happen until several hours later.

The medals had been awarded. The anthems had been played. Even the closing ceremonies had concluded. But as the thousands of attendees stood to gather their belongings and leave the stadium, a voice over the loudspeakers asked that they return to their seats. The race wasn't over yet.

Down the street, motorcycle lights flashed. A lone runner was slowly making his way to the finish line. Spectators watched, curious. After all, the winners had arrived hours earlier. This final racer was John Stephen Akhwari of Tanzania. Early in the race, he'd suffered cramps due to the high altitude. And while trying to improve his position, he'd taken a bad fall that resulted in a bruised head and a lacerated, dislocated knee.

In that moment, his chance at victory died. And he knew it. But after receiving medical treatment, he hobbled back onto the road and continued his race.

As teams, we talk a lot about finishing strong. We emphasize the importance of giving maximum effort until a training session is over, until a rep is complete. On game day, we push through the whistle on every play because wins come to those who persevere. But what about the games we know we've lost? What about those moments when victory passes irrevocably beyond our reach?

Following his marathon, Akhwari was approached by a reporter and asked why he'd chosen to endure such pain when victory was clearly impossible. The runner paused, then answered. "My country did not send me 5,000 miles to start the race. They sent me 5,000 miles to finish the race."

Athlete Huddle

Unpack Akhwari's comment. What would it look like to follow his example in your own life?

Coach Huddle

How might your team's culture change if you made a personal commitment to persevere even when victory seemed out of reach? How could you demonstrate that commitment?

17

The One Percent Rule

Loren Landow

Head Strength & Conditioning Coach/Owner - Denver Broncos/Landow Performance

Whether in sport or business, we often refer to high performers as "The One Percent." People generally associate this seemingly mythical term with an inborn gift that is either physical, such as genetic fiber type, or related to cognitive ability, such as IQ. However, in reality, the concept of the one percent is truly a mindset.

Over the course of my coaching career, I have seen some of the most gifted athletes fail to make the team or advance their career. They've possessed the physical traits, but have lacked something bigger: an ability to maintain both vision and the consistent work ethic needed to produce further growth. I often tell my athletes, "Never sacrifice what you want most for what you want at the moment." This is the rule of discipline, and it is violated often as a result of human nature. A lack of discipline means choosing enjoyment in the short term over what truly needs to be done to achieve one's goal. This short-lived happiness ironically takes us away from our main goal, and ultimately results in self-sabotage.

I have observed countless such cases of self-sabotage. It shows in the athlete who wants to make the team, but stays up all night playing video games; the athlete who wants to earn a scholarship to play college football, but cuts class in high school. It shows in the general population client who wants to look better in a bathing suit, but goes to happy hour every

These examples are everywhere in our surroundings, yet most people do not recognize that they are sabotaging themselves. It is easier to blame others and assume that someone else is luckier or more naturally gifted than we have been, that their success owes to uncontrollable factors. But the truth of the matter is that it merely requires consistency of vision, effort, and values. Approaching life with the knowledge that one can be successful with this type of consistent discipline is a mindset that can make everyone a "one percenter." It is not a genetic gift, and it is not luck. It is a conscious daily decision that influences our thoughts and behaviors, a choice that we all have to make.

Athlete Huddle

Have you ever noticed yourself engaging in self-sabotage? Have you ever felt that others have success or opportunities based on luck?

Coach Huddle

What steps can you take today to avoid "sacrificing what you want most for what you want at the moment?

18

The Wave of Adrenaline

Henk Kraaijenhof

International Performance Consultant - HelpingTheBestToGetBetter.com

One morning during the Olympic Games, I heard a knock at my door. It was one of my athletes. He was due to compete in a semi-final that morning, but he looked terrible. He was pale and trembling, and he told me he'd thrown up. Could he scratch his participation that morning, he asked.

I wasn't worried. I told him, "Haven't you ever seen a Formula 1 race? Do those cars drive straight from the pits to the starting line? No, they do a lap to warm up their tires and engines. That's what is happening to you. Your body is preparing for fight or flight. Your adrenaline is flowing, and that's great."

My athlete was skeptical. Was I really not worried? I repeated that I wasn't. "To be honest," I said, "I'd be more worried if you'd slept well and felt relaxed and bored. It's somewhat early to be warming up already, but I know you'll have enough adrenaline left for the race. Adrenaline is the very best ergogenic aid we know. It's designed to help us survive life-threatening situations. It's your friend, not your enemy. Imagine you're at the beach with your surfboard, and you see a large wave coming in. That wave is adrenaline. It's what you've been waiting for. Some people might shy away out of fear. But you're an expert surfer. Learn to welcome that wave and to ride it."

We ate some light breakfast at the dining hall, and he looked a little better, even after just a few short minutes. "I'm riding the wave, Henk. Can you tell?" To be honest, I could not. But nevertheless, he broke his personal best in that Olympic semi-final.

Athlete Huddle

How do you handle nerves before competition?

Coach Huddle

What is the best thing you can do for your athletes before a big event?

19

One Hundred Paperclips

John Garrish

Director of Athletic Development - North Broward Preparatory School

Our success as teams often depends on our ability to work with each other. As Aristotle said, "The whole is greater than the sum of its parts." This quote has always resonated with me, as a student-athlete and now as a coach. But although we should recognize and respect the roles we occupy, it's important that we don't allow those roles to define us. Who you are as is a person is all that you can give. But all that you can give is not who are as a person.

There's an old story about a paperclip company that conducted a study to find out just how their paper clips were being used. The results surprised them. Of one hundred paperclips, thirty were used as bookmarks. Thirty were used to reinforce jewelry. Thirty were used in arts and crafts. Only ten were used to clip paper, the function for which they were all made!

People are complex. We each bring many things to the table. And as we go through life, we'll probably find that our roles occasionally shift. The role you fill on one team may be different than the role you fill on the next. Being a great point guard isn't the same as being a great father. But the values you learn as a point guard become the values you take into fatherhood. We should never lose sight of our greater purpose. We should always respect and value ourselves as individuals.

Athlete Huddle

How do you describe yourself to others? How do you see your role on your team? What about your role at home, with your family or friends?

Coach Huddle

How does your role inside the weight room align with your purpose as a human being? What are you trying to accomplish with your life?

20

George Bolt

Donnie Maib

Head Coach Athletic Performance - University of Texas at Austin

Years ago, an elderly couple came to a small town late at night, searching for a place to stay. It was raining and cold, and every hotel was fully booked due to a conference that was happening at the time. As the midnight hour passed, they pulled into one last hotel, hoping they'd find a room. When they walked in, a young man at the front desk greeted them. When they asked about accommodations, he explained that they were all full. But because it was so late and the weather was bad, he offered the old couple his own room, explaining that he'd be watching the desk all night. They gratefully accepted and checked out early the following morning.

Several months later, the youth received a train ticket to New York City in the mail, along with a note from the old man, asking him to come and visit. Upon his arrival, the old gentleman met him and explained how impressed he and his wife had been by the young man's service several months earlier. In fact, they were so impressed that they wanted their young friend to manage a hotel they were about to open in New York.

That old gentleman was William Waldorf Astor, and his young friend, who gladly accepted the job, was George Bolt, the first manager of the Waldorf Astoria.

The moral of the story? The way you do your work matters. Embrace the details. Little things make big impacts.

Athlete Huddle

Do you think little things make big differences in sport? Explain.

Coach Huddle

What does excellence mean for you? What are some ways you can show excellence in your job?

22

Two Men On a Train

David Joyce

Head of Athletic Performance -
Greater Western Sydney Giants Football Club

Two men board separate carriages of the same train. It's their morning commute. They take their seats and wait for the train to depart. Except it doesn't.

A moment later, both men look out the window, then glance at their watches. Why hasn't the trained moved? The conductor addresses his passengers via the loudspeaker.

"We apologize for the delay for the delay this morning," he begins. "It appears there's an injured kangaroo on the tracks ahead of us. We're waiting for a ranger to arrive and address the situation. Thank you for your patience. We'll be on our way as soon as the path is clear."

The first commuter hears the message and realizes he's going to be late for his meeting. But what can he do? Nothing. So he opens his newspaper and begins reading.

The second gentleman does not hear the announcement. The speaker in his cabin is broken. He's also running late for an appointment. Increasingly frustrated and confused by the delay, he paces the aisle, indignant.

Eventually, the train moves. Both men arrive at work late, delayed the same amount of the time for the same reason. But there is a marked difference between their moods upon arrival. The first man shows up calm, even happy. He knows he's late, but he's alerted his team. He's also pleased that the kangaroo is safe, which conductor announced shortly before the train departed.

The second man arrives angry, even hostile. He hates being late. More importantly, he hates not knowing why. If only someone had communicated with him.

Just about all conflicts arise from one or both of two issues: misaligned expectations and poor communication. We cannot expect life to proceed without interruption. It never does. But our responses to those interruptions shape the outcomes. If we communicate issues to relevant stakeholders, if we're up front and communicative, we alleviate anxiety for ourselves and others. If a project is off target, acknowledge it. If you want aligned expectations, communicate.

Athlete Huddle

Are you proactive about communicating with your coaches and teammates?

Coach Huddle:

Do your athletes know exactly what you want from them?

23

Reframing Recovery

Nick Winkelman

Head of Athletic Performance & Science - Irish Rugby Football Union

Coaches, here's a way you can demonstrate to your athletes the importance of recovery. After your next session, bring them together and ask the following questions.

When do you perform best, at the beginning of a game or at the end?

They'll most likely say the beginning. That's obvious, right? Less fatigue, more gas in the tank. Now ask this second question.

When are you more likely to hit a PR, at the beginning of a training session or at the end?

Same answer. The beginning. When I'm fresh!

Exactly. Competition, like training, makes us worse in the short-term. It breaks us down. It weakens us. But in the long-term, we reap the benefits of that discomfort. We rebuild. And that leads us to an interesting discovery.

The time we spend recovering before a game is just as important as the game itself. The choices we make when we're not practicing are just as important as those we make when we are. From this perspective, we can consider recovery an insurance policy we take out on our physical investment.

Athlete Huddle

What strategies are you employing to ensure you're maximizing recovery time?

Coach Huddle

It's easy for athletes to approach recovery as recess. How can you effectively communicate to your athletes the importance of respecting the rebuilding process and maintaining discipline in between training sessions?

24

How Will You Remember Your Playing Days?

Micah Kurtz

Director of Sports Performance - Windermere Preparatory School

I want to give you a quick glimpse into my past and your future. For the first 23 years of my life, everything revolved around sports. Weight room, film study, speed and agility work, practice and, of course, games. However, even now, 10 years after my last game as a college football player, my mind often drifts back to those college football days. Playing sports in high school and college have provided some of the absolute best memories of my life. As I think back to those times, the following question often pops into my head: "Was I soft when I played?"

When you think about being "soft," most of you think of a weakling, someone who quits when the game gets tough, someone who is bullied, a player who gets trucked by an opposing running back. That definitely wasn't me. I was a leader on the football field. I hunted wide receivers and running backs. I loved contact. I loved competition and I loved the weight room.

The traditional meaning of the word "soft" is not what I am talking about here. When I ask myself whether I was "soft," I'm really wondering if I was a warrior.

A "warrior" is a person who is true to himself and ignores social pressures. He doesn't feel the need to go out and party. He focuses solely on those things that get him closer to achieving his goals.

If you're "soft," your peers easily influence you. A "soft" person lacks the dedication and discipline to resist temptation. A "soft" person easily goes astray (i.e., shows up to practice hung over, hangs with the wrong crowd, etc.).

The second thing that makes a person "soft" is fear of failure. Fear of failure is natural, but a real "warrior" knows that if he is true to himself, always tries his best and continues to persevere in the face of adversity, he can accept failure without feeling embarrassed. A "soft" person never fully commits, but rather does 90 percent of what it takes or simply never takes the risk of trying something difficult.

Unfortunately, when I ask myself if I was a "soft" when I played, I come to the conclusion that there were several times in my life when I was definitely "soft." There were times when I was influenced by others and partook in activities that prevented me from being the best I could be. In college, I started to drink at parties because alcohol made talking to girls easier. One time, I drank the night before a summer workout and wound up injuring myself while training. Another time, I stayed up all night and ended up missing a workout the following morning.

There were also times when I definitely wasn't "soft." I'm very proud of that. There was the time I skipped spring break with my buddies because I knew spring practice started 10 days after break. I wanted to be ready. I always put in extra work in the weight room and film room. I got great grades in high school for the sole reason that I knew it would make me more attractive to college coaches. I skipped countless parties on Saturday nights during the season, even though many of my teammates went out, because I wanted to be fresh for the upcoming week of practice. In high school, I went to the gym on Saturday nights and worked out or

shot hoops by myself or with my brother, because I knew my competi
was out partying. I knew I was getting better as they were getting worse.
These are things that a "warrior" does.

What I want you to take from this story is that if you do what
everyone else does, or fail to fully dedicate yourself to your true passion, you
will never achieve your dream. You will be average. And if you are truly
passionate about your dreams and goals, but never fully commit to always
doing your absolute best, you will be average; you will be average for the
rest of your life. You will regret that you were not true to yourself, and you
will always wonder how great you could have been. In the years after your
playing days, regardless of how big your house is or how much money you
have earned, you will look back on your playing days and wonder, "Was I
soft?"

How many decisions, instances and moments of truth will you be
proud of? I want you to look back and think, "I was a warrior. I was true to
myself and I didn't fear failure."

Athlete Huddle

When was the last time you let someone negatively influence your
decision?

Coach Huddle:

We all want our athletes to be better than we were. Write down one way
you were "soft" when you played, and use it as a teaching tool.

25

Faith and Belief: Set Your Compass

Gary Schofield

Southeast Director - PLAE

On December 5, 1945, five torpedo bombers took off from an air station in southern Florida. It was a routine training mission that should have been completed in three hours. But none of the planes returned. A rescue was sent after them to investigate. Unimaginably, it never returned either. To this day, no conclusive evidence has ever been brought forward that might explain what happened to those 27 men and their aircraft. The mystery has perplexed scholars for years and fueled theories concerning the Bermuda Triangle.

Whatever the truth may be, this narrative demonstrates the importance of good navigation. A reliable compass is something every pilot needs to succeed. For every degree you fly off course, you miss your target by 92 feet per mile. That means if you were to fly from New York to Los Angeles with a compass that was wrong by one small degree, you'd wind up 50 miles off from your intended destination. Direction matters.

You'll encounter many voices on your journey. Your parents will have opinions. So will your friends, coaches, scouts, trainers, teachers, bosses, etc. Before you embark, make sure your compass is accurate. Otherwise, you risk the likelihood of getting pulled off course.

Athlete Huddle

Do you ever feel like your chasing someone else's mission instead of your own? Do you have someone you trust who can help re-calibrate you when that happens?

Coach Huddle

Have you set your compass by creating a vision and mission statement? How often do you evaluate your actions to ensure they align with your big picture goals?

26

Piggy Bank

Nick Grantham

Performance Enhancement Specialist - NickGrantham.com

Why do most athletes fail to hit their performance goals? Lack of continuity in their training. It seems that many prove incapable of sticking to a plan and prefer the "freestyle" approach.

Training continuity is like depositing money into a piggy bank. If I deposit ten dollars every day for sixty days, I'll have six hundred dollars, right? But if I'm a bit inconsistent and only manage to make deposits on thirty of those days, I'll only have three hundred dollars. Developing a regular training history is going to result in a larger account. It helps you develop your fitness reserves. Developing a good history stands you in good stead for unforeseen time away, maybe due to injury, a holiday, or in preparation for a major competition. Unlike the person who's only built up half a store of fitness reserves, you'll have a full account. You'll be able to afford making withdrawals without going into debt.

Your success or failure as an athlete is dependent on your ability to consistently respect your training plan over an extended period of time. Three weeks of training never made a champion!

Athlete Huddle

Are you prepared to build up your training account before making withdrawals?

Coach Huddle:

Are you consistently investing in your development as a coach? Are you setting that example for your athletes?

27

Inspiration vs. Motivation

Matt Balis

Director of Football Performance - Notre Dame

You guys need to be motivated. You need to be intrinsically motivated. It's up to you to create the mindset needed to be great. What you think and believe about yourself is critical to how you attack everything you do. You have to accept that failure is part of the process. You will fail. That's inevitable. What matters is how quickly you can recover and get back at it.

There's a direct correlation between motivation and action. Our motivation directly affects how hard we are willing to fight to get what we want. And you can be the most motivated person in the world, but there will still be days on which you won't feel like a champion, days when you don't have anything left to give, days when all your motivational thoughts and statements aren't enough to get you through. Then what? What do you do then?

These are the days when having inspiration behind your motivation is so important. Who or what inspires you? Why do you do what you do? Who is it for? Is it God's plan for your life? Does God want you to work as hard as you possibly can towards this goal? If you don't know why you are doing what you're doing, if inspiration isn't there to kick in when your motivation is spent, you'll have a tough time fighting through the really hard days.

You might be asking, "How do I figure out what inspires me?" Well, for starters, what do you think about when you aren't thinking about anything else? When your head hits the pillow, what's on your mind? If you're an athlete, it can't just be the sport. Maybe it's the ultimate goal of success in life, whatever that may look like to you. Whatever it is, you'll know when you come across it. It's an inescapable feeling. You can't satisfy it. You'll think about it all the time. Maybe you haven't found inspiration just yet. That's okay. But I highly suggest you go in search of it.

Athlete Huddle

What is one thing or person you could dedicate this next offseason training program to?

Coach Huddle:

Why do you coach? What is your true purpose?

28

Character

Scott Sinclair

Director of Football Strength & Conditioning - University of Georgia

Hall of Fame football coach Tom Landry once expressed the importance of character by comparing two hypothetical athletes. He said one was naturally talented and achieved success easily. But he lacked the moral fiber that only comes from encountering struggle and rising above it. The second athlete was not quite as gifted, but had undeniable character and work ethic. Which athlete would Landry prefer to have on his team? He said that was an easy question. He'd rather have the second athlete. Why?

Talent is never enough. And without the grit and determination to give maximum effort, talent is useless. Landry said that outstanding athletes who lack character often deliver mediocre effort, which translates into average performances at best. On the other hand, athletes who have depth of character (even if they possess little else) consistently give their all. They push themselves to improve, and they usually do so.

Athlete Huddle

Have I given my max effort on and off the field, court, track, or diamond?

Coach Huddle:

Is it possible to build character in your athletes? If so, how?

29

The Old Man, the Boy and the Donkey

Ron McKeefery

Vice President of Performance & Education - PLAE

An old man, a boy and a donkey were going to town. The boy rode on the donkey and the old man walked. As they went along, a passerby remarked, "What a shame that the boy makes that old man walk."

Maybe he's right, thought the man and the boy. So they stopped and switched places, then proceeded on. Before long, people began to gossip again. "Look how tired the little boy is," they said. "Why would that man make him walk?"

So the man and the boy decided they'd both walk. But once again, their approach was questioned. "Are they stupid? Why aren't they riding that perfectly good donkey?"

That also seemed sensible, so the man and the boy both climbed onto the donkey and continued on their way.

Once again, it wasn't long before someone commented, "How awful to put such a load on that poor donkey." The man and the boy then decided to carry the donkey. But as they crossed a bridge, they lost their grip and the animal fell into the river, where it drowned.

The moral of the story? If you try to please everyone, you might as well kiss your ass goodbye.

Athlete Huddle

Who are some of the outside influences on your playing career, and how have you allowed and/or prevented them from taking control?

Coach Huddle

Has there been a time in your career when you didn't follow your heart and tried to please others instead?

30

Value

Lachlan Wilmot

Head of Athletic Performance/Co-Owner - Parramatta Eels NRL Club/Athletes Authority

Coaches, here's a way you can remind your athletes of their implicit value. Gather them together and hold up a brand new fifty-dollar note. Ask them, "Who wants this? I'm giving it away." All hands go up, right? Who doesn't want free money?

As they watch, crumple up the note and flatten it back out. Hold it up. "Anyone still interested?" That's another easy question. All hands go up again. But you're not quite finished. Drop the note on the floor. Step on it. Scuff it up with your shoe and then hold it aloft once more.

"What about now?" All hands go back up, don't they? Why? The answer is obvious. A fifty-dollar note is worth fifty dollars, regardless of its condition.

I can't overstate the importance of this lesson. Athletes pour their efforts into improving their physical performance. In some cases, they struggle against feeling defined by the degrees of success they achieve. Like the fifty-dollar note, we sometimes crumple under life's pressures. We make bad decisions. We're dealt challenging circumstances that rock us to our cores. We feel worthless.

Let us never forget that no matter what happens in life, we're valuable. We have implicit worth that can't be taken away.

Athlete Huddle

Do you think your injury history defines you? Do you think success has the power to define you?

Coach Huddle:

Do the mistakes you've made as a coach define you? Could you do a better job of demonstrating your respect for human value to your athletes?

31

Lessons from the Banana King

Brett Bartholomew

Strength Coach, Author & Founder - Art of Coaching

J ewish immigrant, Samuel Zemurray, better known later in his life as the "Banana King," changed an entire industry, amassed a fortune that rivaled that of the iconic Rockefeller family, and helped build numerous cultural institutions; all this simply due to his resourcefulness, willingness to get his hands dirty, and ability to exploit what the "experts" didn't recognize.

Zemurray knew that experience was more valuable than exposure as it pertains to gaining a full understanding of a problem and would always make sure to investigate things first-hand as opposed to relying on what others told him was the "truth." He also realized that it didn't pay to try and be "smarter than the problem," meaning that he knew the most efficient path to success was often the simplest or the one right in front of your eyes. Finally, the thing that Zemurray did better than nearly anyone else was act. Even in the face of supreme adversity, which was represented in part by an absolute stalwart of a company in United Fruit, Zemurray was always one step ahead seeking out alternative solutions to every problem in case he needed to pivot.

Athlete Huddle

As competitors, it can be easy to let defining moments become monsters that dwell in our minds. We all have our version of an "against all odds" type of scenario. Name a time when your fear kept you from taking action. What happened and what did you learn from it?

Coach Huddle

Consider a moment in your career when you let enthusiasm, as opposed to pragmatism, sway your thought process. How did enthusiasm make things more complicated and affect your problem-solving ability?

32

A Room Full of Mirrors

Dan John

Coach & Author - DanJohn.net

There's really only one lesson I want my daughters to learn. It flies in the face of what society teaches, but it's nonetheless a cornerstone of personal growth. I hope they learn it soon.

I recently had a conversation with John Smith in which he noted how much his son's mindset had changed since Marine Corps Boot Camp. Gone were the purple hair and nose rings. They'd been replaced by thirty pounds of muscle and a new understanding of community.

Harry Emerson Fosdick once wrote of a young man growing up: "He has lived, let us say, in a mind like a room surrounded by mirrors. Every way he turned he saw himself. Now, however, some of the mirrors change to windows. He begins to get out of himself, no longer the prisoner of self-reflection but a free man in a world where persons, causes, truths, and

values exist, of value for their own sakes. Thus to pass from a mirror-mind to a mind with windows is an essential step in the development of real personality."

When Robert Bellah wrote that seminal study of America, Habits of the Heart, he discovered that most Americans were looking for churches and organizations that seemed more of a support group than a truly Christian community. Bellah's research reflected Fosdick's message. But shouldn't adults be kicking out more mirrors?

It's not about you. It's not about me.

This is one of life's great lessons. But today, we seem to operate on the belief that if something feels good, we should do it. Listen to the loud music coming from the car next to yours at the traffic light? Do you think it occurs to that driver to consider whether others might be annoyed by his music?

It's not complicated. Just kick out the mirrors and open a few windows. It's not about me; it's about us.

Athlete Huddle

Is your mind a roomful of mirrors?

Coach Huddle:

How can we open some windows around here?

33

Greatness Requires Grit

Dan Noble

Director of Athlete Performance - The Hill Academy

My job largely consists of training our nation's brightest young athletes. Most of them have stood out from their peers since an early age. Most of their journeys have been laid out in front of them. Most have never tried out for a team or experienced rejection in their sport. They are your typical generation Z specialized athletes.

Now, I've had several of these kids go on to surpass the success they anticipated. But I've also seen many fall short of what was expected, landing in a frustrated, confused state of disarray, wondering what happened, where they went wrong. Since most of our athletes come to us at early ages (11-12) and stay in our program for 8-10 years, I've been able to spot trends and recognize patterns throughout the process. I've tracked the journeys of those who've made it, as well as those who've not. What's the key difference? Experts identify burnout as a main contributing factor to the failure of those who come up short. But I believe burnout is a symptom of a greater issue. In my opinion, these are the four greatest factors in an athlete's failure.

1. Lack of ability to think independently

2. Inability to respond to increasing pressure and adversity

3. Failure to adapt to new environments or people

4. Overly involved parents

On the other hand, here's my list of key ingredients for a young athlete's success.

1. Extreme awareness of self and what's required to do the job

2. A healthy view of failure as a means of growth and improvement

3. Social adaptability and flexibility to accommodate challenging situations

4. Parents who allow the athletes to make his or her own decisions

The biggest factor here is one's ability to adapt. In athletics, things change constantly, and your aptitude for accommodating an evolving environment is key to your success. Consistently, the kids who succeed are the ones who constantly reinvent themselves. They're the ones who enter every off-season fearless, fully willing to admit their weaknesses and work to correct them. Their approach constantly changes as they evaluate their circumstances and adjust as needed. On the other hands, athletes who resist change struggle. They can't handle new coaches, new positions, new teammates. They've achieved success in specific conditions, and they get irritated when those conditions change. They're inflexible. And when they flounder, they blame others or simply lose confidence in themselves. I've seen this pattern over and over again. That's why I preach to our kids the importance of seeking out uncomfortable situations. They test your ability to adapt, and the more you adapt, the easier you'll be able to adjust when it matters.

Athlete Huddle

What difficult situations do you need to stop running away from and face head on?

Coach Huddle

Do you embrace failure and criticism as a means of getting better, or do you avoid it?

34

Lessons From Geese

Teena Murray

Senior Director of Athlete Health & Performance - Sacramento Kings

Have you ever wondered why geese fly in that famous "V" formation? Study has provided some fascinating insight into why they travel the way they do. Geese operate intuitively as a group to optimize their flock's success. Here are five lessons on leadership and teamwork we can learn from them.

1. By flying in "V" formation, the flock has 71 percent more flying range than it would if each bird flew separately. They all understand the value of pursuing that single goal. They know their individual places. They know each position is important. If we share a common goal as a team, we can achieve it more efficiently by traveling in the wind currents of those around us.

2. When a goose breaks formation, it immediately feels increased wind resistance and struggles to get back in place, where the going is easier. What's our takeaway here? Have the common sense of a goose. Cooperate with the team's direction or you'll make life more difficult for yourself and others.

3. When a lead goose gets tired, it rotates back into formation and another fresher bird takes its place. Too often we let our egos get the best

of us and cling to roles that make us feel important, even though someone else is better suited for the job. It's sensible to take turns doing the hard work involved in leading.

4. Geese in formation honk to encourage the lead goose to keep up the pace. Is our honking encouraging?

5. When a goose gets hurt and falls out of formation, two other geese drop out and follow their comrade to lend help and support. They stay behind until the injured bird either recovers or dies. Then they strike out on their own or join another formation to catch up with their flock. We should always be there for our teammates, in hard times and good. It's the only way to build trust and it's the right thing to do.

Athlete Huddle

How can you adjust your approach to your team to better emulate the wisdom of geese?

Coach Huddle:

How can you adjust your approach to your fellow staff members to better emulate the wisdom of geese?

35

Let Your Game Talk For You

Jerry Palmieri

34 Year Veteran NFL/NCAA Strength & Conditioning Coach

Most NFL teams hold pre-season mini-camps for their rookies. These usually take around three days, during which coaches spend time introducing their new athletes to the unfamiliar system.

As strength and conditioning coach, I'd address this group and orient them to the training protocols they'd follow under my direction. After this orientation, I'd share some wisdom from the Old Testament. In 1 Kings, there's a story of two armies preparing to battle one another. One king sends a message to the other, saying he'll take his wives, children, silver and gold. The threatened king responds, "One who puts on his armor should not boast like one who takes it off." I'd tell these rookies, "As NFL players, you're at the beginning of your careers. You're putting on your armor. Don't talk like you're a seasoned veteran. Don't run your mouth about what you're going to do. You haven't done it yet. Work hard, give your best effort, and do everything you're asked to do. Let your talent shine, not your mouth."

Many times, players arrive in the NFL on the heels of successful college careers. They've been praised by coaches, family members, friends, agents, etc. They have a lot of confidence. And confidence is important! But the process of going pro can sometimes over-inflate a rookie's ego, causing him to think he'll "set the league on fire" with his natural talent. The media catches wind of a comment, and suddenly he's telling the world what he's going to do before he even puts on his uniform. Maybe he'll back up his talk. Usually he won't.

Over the years, I've challenged my athletes with a wise message from Proverbs 27. "Do not boast about tomorrow, for you do not know what a day may bring forth. Let another praise you, and not your own mouth; someone else, and not your own lips." Keep your ego in check. Let your game and your work ethic do the talking for you.

Athlete Huddle

How do you balance confidence and arrogance? Are they the same thing?

Coach Huddle:

Do you find yourself talking about the numbers your athletes are putting up in the weight room and how dominant they'll be during the season? Is that talk beneficial?

36

Everyone Matters

Zach Mathers

Director of Strength & Conditioning/Head Athletic Trainer - University of Sioux Falls

How many letters are in the English alphabet? How many of them matter? Every once in a while, I'll get to thinking that my contribution doesn't make as big of a difference as I like to say it does. Sometimes I'll feel insignificant, like I'm lost in a crowd. Everyone's experienced that, right? We all know what it's like to feel unimportant. But the truth is, everyone matters. There comes a time when the success of any operation, large or small, comes down to one person doing his or her job.

I likx to rxmxmbxr my old typxwritxr and how onx of its kxys stoppxd working at a cxrtain point. That bxcamx frustrating prxtty quickly. How do you fxxl? Insignificant? That doxsn't mattxr. Kxxp doing your job. Bx diligxnt and consistxnt, and rxst assurxd that you play a kxy rolx in your txam's succxss.

Athlete Huddle

What are the details that you've been neglecting?

Coach Huddle:

What's a strategy you could implement that might seem small but would make a big impact on your athletes?

37

Confidence is a Product
of Preparation

Marty Barnett

Director of Strength & Conditioning - Rejoice
Christian School (OK)

David and Goliath. The story is used in motivational speeches by many an underdog coach. But the truth is, David was not the underdog. The outcome, his defeating Goliath, did not surprise David. God prepared David for such a moment as this and David was ready.

When David arrived in the Israelite camp and heard the Philistines cursing his God, David stepped up when no one else would. His preparation and faith gave him the confidence to tell King Saul, "Don't worry about this Philistine...I will go fight him!" David was mocked for his confidence. Was David overconfident, naïve or cocky? Or was David prepared and therefore confident in the outcome?

Preparation breeds confidence. Ray Allen, the greatest three-point shooter in NBA history, was confident because of how prepared he was. Ray said, "My confidence in games comes from my preparation every day in practice and in shoot-around. It is all about being prepared." Ray was confident to take big shots because of preparation. When he was called up to hit a shot, he wasn't thinking about making it. He was prepared to make it.

David didn't waver in his big moment either. In 2 Samuel 17:34-37, David answers King Saul's doubt with confidence in his preparation and in his God. He says, "When a lion or a bear comes to steal a lamb from the flock, I go after it with a club and rescue the lamb from its mouth. If the animal turns on me, I catch it by the jaw and club it to death. I have done this to both lions and bears, and I'll do it to this pagan Philistine, too, for he has defied the armies of the living God! The Lord who rescued me from the claws of the lion and the bear will rescue me from this Philistine!"

When we prepare and are strong in our faith, we can respond during difficult tests. Responding with confidence in the midst of adversity is a product of being prepared. Prepare not to fail.

Athlete Huddle

Does confidence happen by chance or do you have a part to play in your own confidence? How can you speak into your teammates to help prepare them to respond to adversity with confidence?

Coach Huddle:

Are you preparing in your own life to respond with confidence? How does David model the importance of both preparing physically and spiritually?

38

Success

Jeff Nichols

Performance First

I believe we place too much emphasis on winning. One's achievements are commonly considered the only relevant metric, but I disagree. Of course there's value in one's victories, but they are only half of the equation. The other half is made of failure, struggle, loss and heartbreak.

We're all chasing success. We're all chasing improvement. But in the process of pursuing that goal, we undervalue failure. Failure is powerful. It's necessary. I think there may be some confusion between failure and regret. They're not the same. In fact, they're more like opposites. If all we ever do is focus on our wins, we're setting ourselves up for regret, because our approach ignores challenges. Challenges threaten failure, so we sidestep them in order to maintain our winner's narrative. But regret is far darker than failure. It's not as easy to shake off. It's shrouded in shame. It's rooted in fear.

The key is to seek failure. We should be challenging ourselves every day. We should be pushing ourselves every day. We should be stumbling and failing regularly, because only when we truly know our limits can we expand them. This philosophy builds character, which is my ultimate test for my athletes. Character is born in struggle.

I hear people ask why others fail when they've been afforded so much opportunity. Opportunity is sometimes the enemy. It softens us. That's not an advantage; it's an impairment. I always say, "How can we hold someone accountable if they've never been taught what accountability is?"

This world measures outcomes. People care about results. But what is true success? True success is predictable. It's reliable. It's repeatable. Most importantly, it's teachable. It never happens by accident, but rather by a process. Let's stop acting surprised when strong organizations run by strong individuals experience success over long periods of them. They've earned that. It's up to us to cultivate the same culture in our own teams. Victories will follow.

Athlete Huddle

Why are you here and what will you do when you fail?

Coach Huddle:

What do you do when you fail? It's not about blame; it's about solutions. A problem is only a problem when there's no solution. Failure offers solutions, not more problems.

39

The Rhesus Monkey

Matt Nein

Coordinator of Sports Performance - Salisbury University

Back in 1976, an experiment was conducted to study the cultural acquisition of learned behaviors within rhesus monkeys. What's that got to do with you? Let me explain.

The study began when a monkey was placed into a room that contained a treat. As soon as the monkey got close to the treat, its action was negatively reinforced with a blast of air. Eventually, it gave up trying and staying clear of the treat to avoid being punished. At this point in the study, a second monkey is introduced to the room. Naturally, the first thing it does is make for the treat. But then what happens? The first monkey, which has already been conditioned, prevents the second monkey from getting too close to the treat. Over time, the second monkey stops trying, as well.

That's when the first monkey is removed, leaving the second monkey alone with the treat. Now there's nothing standing in its way. Will it take the treat? No. Its learned behavior has taken root. It's been taught the rule, and even though the enforcer is gone, it doesn't approach the prize. It knows better.

"This is how it's always been done." How many times have you heard that? Too often in life, we follow certain approaches because we've been taught to do so. We're not sure what would happen if we didn't, whether the consequences would be good or bad. We just carry on doing what others do, because that's how we were taught.

Athlete Huddle

Do you know why you do what you do?

Coach Huddle:

List five practices you're currently using that you don't fully understand.

40

Want To

Bryan Miller

Associate S&C Coach and Sports Science - United States Naval Academy

After a disappointing 3-9 season, I've done a lot of thinking about why certain athletes seem to play better and recover faster than others, even if there's no measurable difference at play. If two players are the same age, share the same skill level and have the same amount of experience, how does one have a larger impact than the other? I think the answer is what I call "want to." Both players have the same opportunities. But the simple truth is that the one who progresses faster, learns faster, and recovers faster is the one who wants to do so more.

So how do we generate more "want to" in our teams? I like to use a hands-on approach. In my weight room, I have a "want to" buck full of water. When I'm trying to bring this point home for my athletes, I dunk a towel in the bucket and hand it to one of them, instructing them to wring out as much water as they can. When that first athlete thinks he's done all he can, he passes the towel to someone else. And every time, that second athlete manages to squeeze out a few more drops. When he's done, I have him give the towel back to the first kid. And yet again, more water gets squeezed out.

What happened to that first athlete? Did he somehow get stronger while his teammate showed him up? No. He simply engaged his emotions.

He started wanting to. This is a simple principle: creating a competitive environment yields bigger gains.

Athlete Huddle

How can you engage that emotional drive every time you step into a training session?

Coach Huddle:

How many times have you struggled to convince an athlete that he or she has more gas in the tank?

41

The Domesticated Elephant

Anthony Morando

Manager of Human Performance - Altru Health System/EXOS

A man passes several elephants tied to a tree. There's no fence, no chain. There's nothing to keep them from escaping but skimpy ropes tied loosely around their right forelegs, connected to the obliging oak. They could run off at any moment, but they don't. Confused, the man asks a boy who's watering the beasts why they stay where they are. The boy explains that when the elephants are very young, they're tied up using the same ropes that hold them captive now. While immature and weak, the elephants lack the strength to break the rope. So they stop trying. Sure, once they're grown, they can easily free themselves. But they don't know that. In their minds, the rope still imprisons them. And because they never try to break free, perhaps it does.

Like the elephants, how many of us go through life convinced that doing certain things is impossible simply because we tried once and failed? Failure is not final; it's an opportunity to learn. And as we evolve, so does the world around us. Never give up trying!

Athlete Huddle

Do you relate to this story? Do you hold your teammates accountable to persevering when challenges get tough?

Coach Huddle:

Have you ever considered that your lack of buy-in or curiosity might negatively impact the creativity and confidence of your players?

42

Pull the Rope

Mike Srock

Director of Athletic Development - District Five Schools (SC)

A t the core of the Byrnes High Rebel Speed and Strength Program is this concept of pulling the rope. We constantly challenge our teams to "pull the rope" during training sessions, explaining that if you were hanging off the edge of a cliff, tired and about to fall, you'd want someone trustworthy on the other end. Who would that be? The correct answer is every single one of your teammates. Now, that is easy to say, but is it true?

We use three criteria to judge whether an athlete can honestly commit to pulling the rope for his or her teammate.

1. Are you committed? Commitment means chasing excellence in all aspects of life, whether you're in the hallway, cafeteria, weight room, or on the practice field. Commitment means being on time, prepared, focused, and supportive of your team. It means giving your best effort.

2. Can we trust you? Character is what comes out when nobody is watching, and trust is earned by your actions. If you cannot be trusted, you're not committed.

3. Do you care about your teammates? We before me. Do you support your teammates on and off the field, track, court or diamond? Do

you build people up instead of tearing them down? Teammates who truly care about each other make teams that are always successful.

If you can check these three boxes, you pull the rope. And teams that pull the rope win games. We believe in these values so firmly that we've inscribed them onto our lifting platforms.

Athlete Huddle

Evaluate your team's perception of you. Would you pull the rope for them? If so, do they know you would?

Coach Huddle

How can you more effectively set an example for your athletes of pulling the rope?

43

Too Many Mind

Stephen Rassel

Minor League Strength & Conditioning Coordinator - Toronto Blue Jays

In the 2003 film The Last Samurai, Captain Nathan Algren, an American military officer (played by Tom Cruise) gets hired by the Emperor of Japan to train his Japanese army for modern warfare against their Samurai adversary. In his first battle, Algren is captured and detained by the Samurai. While in their encampment, he begins to absorb their culture and combat methods.

Once, while sparring with a warrior who consistently beats him, another Samurai steps forward to offer advice. "Please forgive. Too many mind. Mind the sword, mind the people watching, mind your enemy. Too many mind. No mind."

Because Capt. Algren's attention is dispersed, his primary goal (beating his opponent) is tougher to achieve. Once he takes the warrior's advice, however, choosing to ignore all peripheral activity, choosing to allocate all of his focus toward the task at hand, success comes within his reach. This isn't surprising, is it? We often find ourselves thinking about several things at once while trying to achieve an outcome. In the weight room, on the practice field, etc., peripheral thoughts tend to present themselves. And in many cases, we fail to achieve our goal simply because we're not focused solely on the process of doing so.

Some refer to this ideal state of heightened focus or "no mind" as flow or "being in the zone." It can be an elusive mental space, but those who access it typically unlock better performances in competition than those who do not. I encourage you to take stock of the thoughts crowding your consciousness and to evaluate whether you, like Capt. Algren, have "too many mind."

Athlete Huddle

What are some ways you have left the distractions off the field, in the locker room when you have come to train?

Coach Huddle

When is the last time you have let what is going on outside the weight room affect what happens in the weight room? How can you prevent that from happening again?

44

What I Had I Gave

Jud Logan

Head Track & Field Coach, 4x USA Olympian - Ashland University

Jeep Davis ran for the American Olympic team in 1956 and 1960. He won three gold medals. At a certain 4x400 relay, Jeep was set to run anchor. His team's third exchange was botched, and by the time Jeep recovered the baton, the Americans were well out of contention. But Jeep sprinted like made, racing as though he were in a 200m, closing on the other runners at an unbelievable rate. As they rounded the final turn, Jeep was coming up on the bronze medal team. Giving one last final effort, he leaned into the tape and was awarded fourth place in a photo finish.

After the race, reporters were informed that Jeep had run his anchor lap over half a second faster than the world record. His response was, "I gave what I had."

Give what you have. What you hold back is lost forever.

Athlete Huddle

How can you put yourself in this headspace when a coach asks for your best effort?

Coach Huddle

Does your team understand this mentality?

45

Bees

Whitney Rodden

Head Strength & Conditioning Coach - MidAmerica Nazarene University

The other day, I was listening to a sermon by Joel Osteen in which he told the story of how some astronauts once took bees into space. Several days into their journey, the insects mysteriously began to die off. At first, the scientists were confused. But upon closer study, they realized that the absence of gravity was to blame. You see, bees are designed for resistance. Buzzing their wings keeps them alive. But out in space, the challenge was too easy. They couldn't function without struggle. They couldn't survive.

In a way, we're like those bees. We're made to fight gravity. When life is easy, we don't mature. We don't develop. Why then, if we know this to be true, do we still seek the path of least resistance? You'll never grow if you don't encounter hardship. You'll never get stronger if you stop challenging yourself in the gym. If you don't increase the weight or the number of reps, if you don't push yourself physically, you'll stay the same. My challenge to you is to embrace struggle, both physically and mentally. Seek it out. Leave your comfort zone. It can make all the difference in establishing your future success.

Athlete Huddle

Do you look for the path of least resistance when you train, or do you push yourself to your limits?

Coach Huddle

Are you searching for ways to challenge yourself emotionally?

46

Wishing for Your Time Back

Brian Clarke

Head Strength & Conditioning Coordinator - Noblesville High School (IN)

I t's Friday. 7:30 pm. The stadium is packed and electric. You are so excited to perform in front of your hometown, family, and friends. Everyone is pulling for you. You've been waiting for this moment, this opportunity, your entire life. It's what you've dreamed of and prepared for. Everyone keeps saying, "You've got this!" No one has worked harder than you. You deserve this. It's game time. Soon, the emotion and energy wear off and before you realize it, the buzzer sounds and the game is over. Defeated.

You're exhausted. You believe you gave it your all, that you had prepared as best you could. But the end result told you otherwise. An array of emotions floods your mind, body and soul. You can't seem to grasp why this happened. As you now sit in the locker room and rethink all of the game's smaller details, it hits you like an 18-wheeler. You realize what you failed to do. You can't believe you let something like this stand in the way of success. Now you sit there numb, wishing you could go back and have a redo, wishing you could get your time back.

Every one of us has had defining moments in our performances that make us wish we could turn back the clock and make a different choice.

We wish we had worked harder at practice or in the weight room, watched more film, slept more, monitored nutrition and hydration, displayed higher character, held onto the ball a little tighter, swung the bat, run harder, listened more carefully, worn that protective piece of equipment, responded more effectively, embraced the process, and on and on.

So now, you are laying in the locker room in utter disbelief. You become even more frustrated, knowing what you needed to do differently. You would do anything to have that time back. To make matters worse, you hear in the background a loud, nerve-racking noise. It's that noise you dread every morning. All of a sudden, you frantically sit up only to find yourself in bed. It's Friday morning. 6:30 am. You were dreaming. You get up so excited because you now know what to do to be successful. Your wish came true. You have your time back. Now, go use it wisely.

Athlete Huddle

List 3 moments as a student-athlete that you wish you could redo. How could you have prepared differently for those moments? What can you do in your weekly preparation process to ensure you perform at your highest level?

Coach Huddle

What are some defining moments in an athlete's career? How can you better prepare yourself, your staff and your athletes for those upcoming challenges? Are you starting with the end result in mind?

47

The Student and the Master

Stu Roche

Assistant Director of Sports Performance - Marquette University

A young student of Zen finds his master meditating and addresses him. "Please, Master," he begins. "Might I ask you a question?"

"Go on," replies the aged teacher. The student clears his throat.

"If I remain diligent and steadfast, how long will it take me to find Zen?"

The teacher thinks, then responds. "Ten years."

"What if I practice every day and apply myself more than my peers? How long then?"

Once again, the teacher ponders the question. "Twenty years."

The student appears confused. "But what if I study harder than anyone has ever studied?"

"Thirty years."

"Master, I don't understand," the youth objects. "Each time I say I'll work harder, you say it will take me longer. Why?"

His master looks up. "Because when you have one eye on the goal, you only have one eye on the path."

Athlete Huddle

Is the teacher's response counterintuitive? Do you agree with him?

Coach Huddle

Where is your focus as a coach, on a desired outcome or on the process?

49

The Farmer and the Mule

Scott Bennett

Assistant Athletic Director for Sports Performance - Radford University

A farmer had an old mule that fell into a deep, dry well and began to cry loudly. Looking down at the trapped animal, he mopped his forehead and considered how difficult, nigh impossible, it would be to rescue it. Because the mule was old and the well was dry, the farmer fetched his shovel, planning to bury the animal in the well.

He called upon his neighbors to help him and they agreed. To work they went. Mounds of dirt began to fall on the mule's back. He became hysterical. But then, the mule did something unexpected. Each time they would throw a shovelful of dirt on his back, he would shake it off and pack it down, raising himself up, inch by inch. Shovelful after shovelful, the mule would shake it off and step up. Exhausted and dirty, but quite alive, the mule eventually stepped over the top of the well and walked through the crowd.

This is a story I tell our kids when adversity strikes. Even though you may feel like you can't overcome the problem in front of you, even though you may feel like there's no way out, there is always an answer. Shake it off and step up. The load you carry may feel overwhelming, but if you can shake it off, one shovelful at a time, and step up, one step at a time, there is no amount of adversity you can't overcome.

Athlete Huddle

Are you ready to quit?

Coach Huddle

When facing adversity, how can keep the "big picture" in view and get the student-athletes over their first hurdle in the process of defeating adversity?

50

Two Monks On a Walk

Ashley Jones

25+ Years Professional Strength & Conditioning Coach

Two monks are walking along together, an elder and his pupil. They come to a stream, where they encounter a young maiden stranded. She wishes to reach the opposite shore, but the water is too high. The elder monk immediately offers to help. He picks her up and wades across, where his pupil meets him and they continue on their way.

As they go along, the elder senses resentment in his young companion. Tension builds. Several hours pass, and their conversation wanes. The old monk pauses and asks his pupil what is wrong, whereupon the boy launches into a tirade, condemning his teacher for breaking the rules of their order in helping the girl.

The elder looks upon his companion lovingly, thanks to him for his passion, and says, "I put the young lady down some three hours ago. Why are you still carrying her?"

Athlete Huddle

Do you spend more time looking forward or back?

Coach Huddle

How do you respond to immaturity? Do you ever mistake misapplied passion for insubordination?

51

The Wolf

Evan Simon

Head Strength & Conditioning Coach - Davidson College

The strength of the pack is in the wolf, and the strength of the wolf is in the pack.

As a coach in today's athletic world, it's easy to focus solely on yourself, to become caught up in your own personal goals and visions. The recruiting process can be more about hearing and structuring what you want than selling and understanding the concept of team. That's why I greatly appreciate the statement above as a way to express the importance of togetherness and what a strong-minded, hard-working group of young men or women can accomplish.

Being a lone wolf can be intimidating, but a pack of wolves working together can take down obstacles, achieve big goals, and see their collective vision take shape. I use this example with the teams I serve as a way to paint a picture of teamwork. Even though you can achieve things by yourself in life, the ability to share a vision and carry it out with others can be much more impactful and rewarding. In a team setting, one person's actions can greatly affect the whole. But when those people are all working toward the same goal, they can hold onto that community experience and refer back to the principles behind it throughout their lives. Understanding the power of team and togetherness, trusting in your relationships with others, is what sport should be about.

Athlete Huddle

What can you do to improve yourself as a wolf and raise the expectations of your pack?

Coach Huddle

How can you demonstrate to your athletes the symbiotic power of the pack concept?

52

The One-Armed Wrestler

Brian Bert

Head Strength & Conditioning Coach - University of North Florida

There was a boy born with only one arm. As he grew older, he became very active and loved sports, but was always limited by his arm. His favorite sport was football but his mother wouldn't let him play. He finally convinced her to let him try wrestling.

When he joined the wrestling team, his coach taught him one move. They drilled the move over and over again for three months. His coach then turned to him and said, "I think you're ready to enter a tournament." The boy was very excited, however, a little hesitant. After all, the coach had only taught him the one move. The coach told the boy to trust him. With the skills he'd learned, he'd be okay. So, he entered the tournament.

He won his first match, then his second. He went on to win his third and made it all the way to the finals of the competition. The opponent he was set to face was far more experienced than he was. He had won all his matches and injured a majority of the competitors he went up against. The referee approached the one-armed boy's coach and asked if he was sure he wanted to enter his athlete into this match, being that he was already at a disadvantage with one arm in addition to the opponent being extremely talented. The coach simply replied, "yes."

Again, the boy was more reluctant, not understanding why his coach had only taught him one move. The coach talked to the boy and told him he would be fine if he just went out there and executed the move they'd been working on. The boy did. And he won the tournament.

On the car ride home, the boy turned to the coach and yelled, "Coach, why would you put me out there unprepared only having learned one move? I could have gotten seriously injured"

The coach looked at him and said, "The only way to stop that move is to grab your right arm."

Athlete Huddle

Are you bought into the process? Do you trust the process?

Coach Huddle

How often do you feel like your athletes don't see the big picture? Can you do a better job explaining to them what you are doing as well as why they are doing it?

53

The Prize is in the Process

Ryan Davis

Head Strength Coach - Colorado State University

In this day and age, too many people want to get the prize without the process; they have the "microwave mindset." People want to put things in the microwave for 30 seconds and see the finished product. Think for a second. Before microwaves, the most efficient way to heat something up was an oven. The oven required time. It required patience. There was a process. And if we're being honest, most of the time, the food was better than the microwave version.

Today, we battle a sense of entitlement with athletes. They are often impatient, having everything at their fingertips. We live in a world where things are quick. They don't require a great deal of work or patience. In my opinion, this lack of patience and process breeds entitlement and a need for immediate gratification.

I have been working for Coach Bobo for the last three seasons and the thing we always tell our team is that the prize is in the process. I give credit to Jocko Willink for providing what we feel is the perfect metaphor to describe what our program is about: pushing the rock.

People want results without the strain. We want our athletes to embrace the strain. Imagine taking a rock and having to push it up a mountain, one grueling step after another. There are lessons to be learned with every step. You see, it's not about getting to the top. It is simply about focusing on putting every ounce of you into the next step. Every day brings new challenges, and regardless of the challenges, we have to be willing to put everything we have into pushing that rock just one more step. Every single time a new challenge is thrown at you and you overcome it by pushing the rock one more step, there is a certain growth that happens internally which makes the next challenge just a little bit easier to push through.

When you learn to embrace the process of pushing through those daily challenges, you will callous your mind and spirit in a way that you can face adversity head on and not fold or flinch when it hits. That, my friend, is the prize. We try to impart this knowledge to every one of our athletes because it prepares them for the road ahead. If you can get a team to focus this way, day in and day out, and the right opportunity meets the process, you may be playing or competing for championships on a consistent basis. More importantly, you know you are preparing your athletes for the challenges they will face in the real world. Keep pushing the rock.

Athlete Huddle

What are some things you are going to have to find a way to push through?

Coach Huddle

What will you do today to get your athletes to push and take that one step to get better?

54

Pumpkins

Ryan Johnson

Director of Strength & Conditioning - Wayzata High School (MN)

I went to a small high school. My parents taught there, so I knew everyone and they knew me. Halloween of my senior year, my friends and I drove around town gathering pumpkins, which we then smashed all over the sidewalk of the school's entrance. I remember us laughing hysterically as we did so. The following morning, we showed up expecting to see our handiwork, but the pumpkins were all gone. The custodians had shown up early as usual and cleaned up our mess, much to our disappointment.

I wrapped up my senior year and managed to secure a job at the school that summer. Graduation was on a Thursday. I strutted across the stage to accept my diploma, feeling pretty good about myself, and rocked the weekend before arriving for work Monday morning, bright and early.

Donnie, the head custodian, ushered me to the gym for my first assignment. As he unlocked the doors, I saw that nothing had changed since Thursday night. "I guess you can start by cleaning up after your party," he said. You could say that reality set in pretty quickly that summer. Regardless of what I'd accomplished so far, I wasn't getting anything more without earning it.

That was a great summer. Towards the end of it, Donnie asked me to clean up some vines that had overgrown the shrubs at the school entrance. It was messy work. When he came to check on me later, he asked if I knew what they were. I said I had no idea. He chuckled and told me, "Pumpkins."

Athlete Huddle

What kind of consequences are you creating for your future self?

Coach Huddle

How do you determine the way you treat your individual athletes?

55

It's All About Effort

Bob Alejo

Director of Sports Performance - Power Lift

Okay, look at me. Today was a great day. We got better. Here's what I liked about today. Here's how we improved: I saw a lot of concentration at the platforms, heavy weights being lifted, and you encouraging one another. I saw really strong folks encouraging teammates with less strength than themselves, as if only the effort mattered and not the weight. I gave you the workout, you followed what I asked you to do, and I can honestly say that today has been the best you've put forth so far.

Remember, and I tell my own children this: "It's all about the effort!" Really, when you think about it, it's the only thing you can control: how hard you try. Results are secondary to me because without effort, results are impossible anyway. If you go as hard as you can, lifting, practice, school, and you meet up with a momentary disappointment, you tip your hat and come back to fight another day. If your effort is poor, short or unfocused, you will never know what could have been. After today, your body and mind will not be the same. Tomorrow, because of the intensity you put into today, you will have a body and mind you never had before. Get ready for it. I'm excited for you.

This is where we can improve: the tempo, the pace of our work. Still a bit short. Things happen a bit faster at this level, and I want you to be prepared for it. Know what weight you want on the bar before your set. Partners, help load and unload the bar immediately after your set for your teammate. Small things, not much, but enough to make a difference.

Now, listen to me. Think of yourselves as champions every day. The way you walk, the way you dress, the way you study, the way you go about your business. Most importantly, hold your teammates to the same standard. I was a coach on the 2006 NCAA National Championship men's soccer team from UC Santa Barbara. In January of 2006, the beginning of spring quarter, they made sure they referred to themselves and their teammates as champions every day, as many times as they could. After practice, conditioning or a weight training session, we always broke it down with the cry of "Champions!" You could see the commitment grow as the view of that goal came into focus, and when August arrived, it was all too real. During the season, it became that much more intense. No talk of winning the conference, or any number of matches. No talk of what seed they wanted in the tournament. No discouragement after a loss. Only the intention of winning the national title. Did it work? I don't know. The one thing I know for sure is this: they called themselves "champions" every day, and in double-overtime in the snow, they became champions.

Hold yourself to that same standard and good things will happen. Go and have a great day!

Athlete Huddle

How do you describe yourself? How do you see yourself?

Coach Huddle

What does it mean to be a champion? What kind of champions do you want your athletes to be?

56

The Importance of Staying Sharp

Greg Werner

Senior Director of Strength & Conditioning Women's Basketball - Virginia Tech University

A strong young man desired to become a lumberjack, so he went to the forest and observed the techniques of the best woodcutters. He studied how they pulled their axes back and how they used their hips and torsos to create speed and power on their blades. He watched them succeed.

After several hours, the young man left to find a private spot in the woods where he could hone his skills. He practiced until he felt confident that he could keep up with the veteran lumberjacks. Returning to the camp the following morning, he approached the foreman and asked for a job.

"Let's see you fell a tree first," the foreman offered. The young woodcutter grabbed an axe and did as instructed with remarkable skill and speed. The foreman scratched his head, impressed. "You're hired! Grab a fresh axe and start immediately."

Excited, the young man worked hard all day. When the bell rang, he'd chopped more lumber than anyone else in the camp. The foreman approached to congratulate him. "You're our top woodcutter today. Keep up the great work!"

The next day, the young man determined to do even better. He showed up early and applied himself all day. But by quitting time, he'd fallen to second place. On Wednesday, he worked even harder, but by Thursday, he'd dropped all the way to the bottom of the board. Confused by his poor performance, the woodcutter took a special supplement to boost his energy levels and decided to work longer than anyone else the following day. He showed up early and chopped like a madman all morning. Midway through the afternoon, the foreman approached and told him to pick up his check. The young man couldn't believe his ears. "You're letting me go?"

"I'm afraid so," the foreman continued. "Your productivity is way down." Disappointed, the woodcutter returned to the camp and collected his pay.

"Sir, I'm so confused," he finally admitted. "I did well my first day, but since then my performance has only worsened. And I can't work any harder! What am I missing?" The foreman sat in silence for a moment, thinking.

"You've been sharpening your axe each morning?"

The young man didn't understand. "Sharpening my axe? No, I've been too busy chopping wood!"

The foreman shook his head. "You never noticed how the older men showed up early each morning to file their blades?"

"I guess I was just focusing on trying to beat them," the woodcutter admitted. "I should have paid more attention to what they were doing to prolong their success."

Here's the point. We as coaches can easily fall into the same trap as the woodcutter. We can become so fully absorbed in grinding toward our goals that we forget to pause and sharpen our axes. We neglect the habits that ensure long-term success. Consider the various aspects of your life:

120

mental, physical, emotional, spiritual, social, etc. These are the axes in your shed. Invest in keeping them sharp. If they become dull, you may wind up working harder for fewer gains.

Coaches and athletes should take a few minutes each morning and evening to sharpen their axes. That could mean reading a book, consuming other sorts of educational material, or simple self-evaluation. Keep your body healthy. Keep your spirit fed. Keep developing your skills. Study the techniques of those more advanced than you are. Know where to focus your energy. Know how to invest in long-term success. You owe yourself a sharp blade.

Athlete Huddle

Do you need to sharpen any of your axes? Are you wasting energy on swinging any dull blades?

Coach Huddle

Do you approach your job as a sprint or a marathon? Are you investing in keeping all of your blades sharp?

57

Alarm Clock

Matt Nein

Coordinator of Sports Performance - Salisbury University

When the alarm clock goes off in the morning, what do you do? How many of you hit the snooze button for 5 more minutes of rest? How many of you hop up and get going? If I gave you two general scenarios for your day, I wonder which you'd choose.

1. Tired, sluggish, groggy, fatigued throughout the day

2. Rested, energized, motivated, ready to attack the day

I can't imagine anyone choosing the first of the two scenarios. Can you? Oftentimes, people don't realize the effect that attitude and mindset have on their lives. See, how you start your day will undoubtedly affect the outcome of your day. By getting straight out of bed and not hitting snooze, you subconsciously adopt the mindset to attack the day. Getting started this way, your day is often full of energy and motivation to be great and to make each day better than the last. Alternatively, delaying the start of your day can set you on a path of negativity that will take effort to overcome. Along with the negative scientific aspects related to hitting snooze (disrupted circadian rhythm, poor sleep quality, lack of sleep affecting recovery), starting your day off with such pessimism is going to test your willpower when it comes to achieving greatness. My challenge to you is to start your day off on the right foot. Put them on the floor, get up, and attack each day with an attitude of greatness.

Athlete Huddle

What strategies can you use to attack the day and not hit snooze?

Coach Huddle:

What immediate benefits in your life might occur if your mindset was geared to attack the day?

58

Countering That Voice

Tyler Carpenter

Head Strength & Conditioning Coach (Olympic) - University of Pittsburgh

An athlete came into the weight room for a quick stretch. She was extremely nervous about running her first 600 meter at the Conference Championship level. She had run countless 600s in training and in high school track meets, had run much longer distances, and had even run the 400 in college. Despite all this great race experience, she kept repeating that she was "so nervous to run the 600 meter at a conference meet."

I asked her a simple question: "How many 600s do you think you've run in your life?" She laughed and said hundreds. By opening that door, I knew I could use a self-talk technique called countering in which you overcome negative self-talk and fears with rational thoughts and facts about previous experiences of success and preparation. Without having to say much more, the athlete realized she had been in this position so many times before and had championed the races and workouts. Nerves before big workouts or long training runs were always much ado about nothing. She recognized she needed to focus on the process and the outcome would take care of itself.

Before loading the bus just a few hours later, she told me she felt so much less pressure realizing that it was just like running a workout with a big audience watching. If she could run a 400, 800 or 1500 meter on big stages, why couldn't she run a 600? She went on to make finals and take fourth place in the conference after being seeded outside of the top ten.

Simple conversations with athletes you have built rapport with can go a long way. They begin to believe in themselves as they believe in your coaching. I didn't even need to get into the specifics of self-talk or techniques of it. She was able to grasp it for herself and find success.

Athlete Huddle

Think about a time you've felt uneasy about a practice or contest. Does remembering that experience make you feel less anxious about future competitions?

Coach Huddle

Have you ever thought to yourself, Why can't my athlete break through this confidence issue? Are you equipped with techniques and mental skills to help them overcome it?

59

Stop Crying

Carmen Bott

Sports Performance Consultant & Professor of Kinesiology

Years ago, when I was a rookie S&C coach, I worked with a guy named Tad. One night, we were coaching a group of hockey players together and he asked me to run a portion of the workout. I was a bit flustered and felt put on the spot. I always like to be prepared. Instead of offering help or guidance, Tad focused his attention elsewhere, leaving me to sink or swim. I was left to my own devices, feeling unsure of what to do and what was expected of me.

The next morning, I arrived at the training facility and opened up my email. I found a message written about me, by Tad, to my boss. I guess I had been accidentally blind copied. The email stated that I didn't know what I was doing and that the workout the night before was terrible and poorly led. I felt my heart sink and my stomach turn. Then I began to cry.

I sat there, feeling shameful and sorry for myself, and I picked up the phone and called my dad. I needed support and validation. I'm not a terrible coach! Or am I? My dad was at work and he answered his direct line. "Don speaking!" he bellowed in a stern voice. "Dad, can you talk?" Through endless tears and a shaky voice, I explained to him the email I had found.

He listened.

Instead of telling me he understood and that everything was going to be okay, he took a very different tone. He said this. "Carmen, stop crying." He was calm and level as he spoke. "You go find your boss and ask to have a conversation about this. You tell him this is unacceptable workplace etiquette. But first, stop crying."

I was surprised at first by my dad's advice. I thought for sure I would get empathy and support. What I did not know at the time was that this was my first real-world lesson in being a problem solver. He didn't let me wallow in self-pity. Instead, he gave me my power back and advised me on an action plan.

He enabled me and empowered me to fix my own situation. Needless to say, the meeting with my boss went very well. Athletes must learn to be problem solvers and solution seekers. Wallowing in self-pity and playing the victim doesn't get you anywhere. Instead, wipe those tears and get after it.

Athlete Huddle

When was the last time you felt defeated? How did you get past it? What did you learn from that experience?

Coach Huddle

How should a leader handle rejection? What about embarrassment? What's the most important thing to remember in those situations?

60

The Bank Account

Al Johnson

Director of Football Strength & Conditioning

Preparing for the future requires careful management of your time. This is true in both life and sport.

Imagine you had a bank account that generated $86,400 every morning. Suppose that every night, the balance fell back to zero, causing you to lose whatever you didn't spend. What would you do? You'd withdraw every cent, right?

The truth is, each of us has an account like this. It's called time. Every morning, it credits us with 86,400 seconds. Every night, whatever hasn't been used goes to waste. These accounts carry no balance. There's no overdraft allowance. Once time is gone, there's no getting it back. There's no borrowing from future deposits. There's only today, right now.

The good news is that we and only we decide how we spend the time we're given. We can spend on whatever we choose. And we get what we pay for. So make the most of today! The clock is ticking. Spend your seconds wisely. Invest them.

Yesterday is history. Tomorrow is unknown. Today is a gift.

Athlete Huddle

Are you managing your time on and off the field to help point your team toward success?

Coach Huddle

Are you investing your time in things that will last a long while? Are you investing in things that matter?

61

Leadership Is Earned

Zach Mathers

Director of S&C/Head Athletic Trainer - University of Sioux Falls

What gives someone the right to lead? A promotion? A title? A rank or degree? No, not even an election. Not even years of experience. Leadership cannot be given. It cannot be taken. It cannot be assumed. It can only be earned. And that takes times. You can pick team captains, but you can't pick leaders. Leadership emerges.

The key to becoming a leader is to not persuade others to follow. It lies in becoming someone they want to follow. Make yourself trustworthy. Make yourself consistent.

A leader serves. He's not too good to get dirty. He puts others first. A leader stands at the front. He's the first into battle, the first to embrace danger. He never orders someone else to take a risk he wouldn't. A leader sees himself as a team player, not a general. He works alongside others, not above them. He celebrates victories as results of team effort. A leader is a builder. The more confidence he constructs, the more creativity he encourages, the more successful his team. He never tears down. A leader not only lays plans but takes action. He's not afraid of being imperfect. A leader leads and a leader can be led. A leader embraces good ideas, even if they challenge his own.

Athlete Huddle

What did I leave out? What makes a good leader? What leadership qualities do you see in your coaches?

Coach Huddle

How can you better serve your fellow coaches?

62

Activity vs. Achievement

Bryan Fink

Co-Director of Sports Performance - Eastern Michigan University

M any times in sport, coaches and athletes think it's all about getting the work done, knuckling down and knocking it out. If I want to be a better shooter, I need to get off 1,000 shots per day. If I want to be faster, I have to be doing sprint work each day. If I want to drive the golf ball harder, I've got to hit three bags of ball every day.

I'm not saying there's no value in this approach. But in order to derive maximum benefit from it, you've got to respect correct execution and prescription. John Wooden said, "Do not mistake activity for achievement." I've seen so many athletes dragging themselves through the motions, mentally disengaged, instead of attacking a movement with specific intention. This is usually apparent during repetitive activities that are executed daily. Intention is key. If you're body's laboring but not your mind, you're not deriving maximum benefit from your work. Focus on achieving something. Focus on improving. Attack your training with a goal in mind. Don't just do the work. Try to do the work as perfectly as you can.

Athlete Huddle

When was the last time you felt yourself going through the motions? What strategies could you implement to keep that from happening?

Coach Huddle

How can you help your athletes avoid mindless repetition? What can you do to emphasize the importance of mindful training?

63

Cemetery

Michael Doscher

Head of Speed/Strength & Conditioning - Valdosta State University

The view from our weight room windows is of our city's cemeteries. So over the years, I have used that view as an avenue to talk about several mindsets.

The first mindset is a complainer mindset. When my athletes start complaining about stupid stuff, I bring them over to the window and tell them to go out the door and jump the fences. They look confused and ask me why. I tell them that it's the complaint department and to go find someone over there that will give a damn about their complaints. They would gladly trade places with the living. The athlete realizes that his or her complaining is small and petty and they move forward and work harder.

The second mindset is an arrogant mindset: when they start feeling bigger than their britches. I walk them over to the window and ask them how many people over there felt invincible at one time and look where they are now. We only have one life. We have to stay humble and do our best. We will all die one day, no matter how good we are.

The third mindset is a lazy mindset. I use the cemetery to show these athletes that time is ticking away on all their dreams and goals. We

13

Do It Anyway

Lew Caralla

Head Football Strength & Conditioning Coach - Georgia Tech University

Peeople are often unreasonable, irrational, and self-centered. Forgive them anyway. If you are kind, people may accuse you of having selfish, ulterior motives. Be kind anyway. If you are successful, you will come across some unfaithful friends and genuine enemies. Succeed anyway.

If you are honest and sincere, people may deceive you. Be honest and sincere anyway. What you spend years creating, others can destroy overnight. Create anyway. If you find serenity and happiness, some may be jealous. Be happy anyway. The good you do today will often be forgotten. Do good anyway. Give the best you have and it will never be enough. Give your best anyway.

In the end, your actions are between you and God. It's about what he knows, not what they think they know.

This is one of the best jolts of perspective I've ever been able to give our players. It reminds them that even though we live in a competitive and jealous world, we need to focus on the bigger picture. It's not about you vs. them. It's about doing what's right anyway. When you are great at something, all kinds of critics will try to bring you back down to their level. Be great anyway.

Athlete Huddle

Why do you persevere? What's your goal? What role does personal integrity play in that equation?

Coach Huddle

When was a time when you felt jealous of someone else because you were constantly comparing yourself to them?

101

Dedicate Your Actions

David Jack

Owner-Activprayer

My old defensive coordinator was college position coach to Deion Sanders. When I asked him about Deion (thinking prima donna), he said, "That kid was the hardest working player I ever coached at FSU. If I asked him to run through a brick wall, he would ask where and how many times." I was floored. I'd expected a totally different answer (judging a book by its cover is a lesson for another day). Fifteen years later, however, it all started to make sense.

During his 2011 Hall of Fame acceptance speech, Sanders alluded to his mother. To paraphrase, he said that she was always an incredibly hard worker, but it had never really gotten her very far. He remembered feeling mad and embarrassed by her struggle to make ends meet. He'd thought about how he could make life better for her. All he knew at a young age was that he could play football. So he made a vow to become the best football player in the country.

All of a sudden, my defense coordinator's story began to add up.

Though Deion loved the sport, the fame and the money to an extent, those things were never powerful enough drive him to work as hard as he did. His pursuit of success in football was paved by what we call "activprayers", actions dedicated to intentions beyond self. These actions are inspired and inspiring. They catch people's eyes, hearts and souls. Many saw Deion as a showboat, an egotistical superstar. Maybe that's part of who he was. But many didn't realize his dedication to a greater cause (his mom's wellbeing) that truly drove him to be one of the best football players of all time, as well as one of the

hardest workers in the weight room and on the practice field. With each play, each rep and each yard, he honored his mother's life. He sacrificed for her wellbeing. He justified the struggle she'd endured.

Could this be you? Each time you step into the weight room, up to the bar, onto the field or court, you have the opportunity to dedicate that set, rep, run or play to something greater than yourself: a friend you're grateful for, someone who's sick and suffering, a tragedy in your community, a mission that's changing the world, or maybe a younger sibling who's looking to you for life cues.

What can you carry with you into the gym today? Dedicate a rep, a set, or the whole workout to something that truly matters and see what effect that has on the effort you pour into what you're doing.

Athlete Huddle

Can you share a greater intention that might full greater effort in yourself or your teammates?

Coach Huddle

What fuels your desire to be the best coach in the world? Is it something that truly matters? Why?

21

It's Not About the Podium

Dan Pfaff

Owner - Pfaff Sports Consultancy

"Sticks" Smith was 5'7" and 140 lbs. He was a local kid with absolutely no leg speed and a very limited skill set for his event, the pole vault. But the high school he'd attended was well known and respected, and his coach was a local legend who'd graduated from our university. I remember our squad was looking good that year. There was no need for us to lower our standards, but Smith's coach and academic advisor had been hammering me nonstop to meet the kid and accept him as an invited walk-on athlete. So I met him and his parents at one of our last outdoor meets. His passion impressed me. So I gave in and invited him onto the team. Also, his academic record was excellent, so I figured that at worst, he could mentor the other guys on our team who struggled in the classroom.

I never regretted my decision. "Sticks" was always the first to arrive and the last to leave. He'd pick up trash after every session, load the team bus for our equipment manager, and carry bags for our trainers. Never once, during his whole four-year career, did he ever ask for anything. Moreover, "Sticks" was an extreme student of his event. He watched hours of film, intelligently questioned all of our training decisions, and relentlessly focused on improving everything we defined as a KPI.

In his senior year, we encountered some injuries on the team, and "Sticks" wound up being the last guy named to our conference outdoor roster. In four years, he'd never made that list. He was so excited, I thought he'd hurt himself during that last week of training.

When we got to the meet, the weather was absolute crap. Two of my better athletes failed to clear the opening height. "Sticks" showed up to compete. He made several heights on his last attempt and somehow wound up finishing 6th in a very strong league for pole vaulters. Watching him that day was the highlight of my spring and probably the highlight of his athletic career.

Athlete Huddle

Many claim to be all in, but how hard will you strive to achieve the goals you've put in place?

Coach Huddle

What are the core values that drive you in your career?

can't waste a day thinking we have tomorrow. We are not promised tomorrow. We must make the best of today. I remind them that their talents are God-given and what a waste it would be not to develop their gifts. They must make the most of their training and gifts before their time runs out.

Athlete Huddle

Do you find yourself getting into one or more of these mindsets at times? How do you get out of them? Are you helping your fellow teammates when they struggle with complaining, arrogance or laziness?

Coach Huddle

You may not have a graveyard handy, so how do you address these three mindsets in your athletes?

64

Three Golden Rules

Ted Perlak

Associate AD for Sports Performance/Head S&C Coach - University of Delaware

I've always tried to give my staff guidance on how to stay even keel and objective when issues arise. As we all know, there are times when stress levels climb pretty high and we'd all benefit from taking a step back and a deep breath.

What follow are three rules I share with my team for such moments, and although

they might come across as slightly negative, they really aren't. Sometimes, a little humor can help equalize a charged situation and bring back healthy perspective.

1. Student-athletes lie. The vast majority of issues that occur in communication come from this simple fact. And as former student-athletes ourselves (as many of us were), I think we can all agree that the truth gets stretched from time to time. It's usually not malicious, but rather convenient. It saves them getting called out or extra work, etc. I always tell my staff to take the first conversation with a grain of salt. Circle back later on when their guard isn't up.

2. Sport coaches are crazy. This one comes with the territory, and it makes sense. I think you have to be a little bit crazy to place your livelihood

in the hands of college kids. So when a coach is fired up and asking for the latest, greatest training movement or warm-up, just hear them out and take it in. You'll have a chance later on to sit down with them and leverage their ideas toward developing the best program possible for their athletes.

3. Administrators are scared. This can be hard to explain to young staff members. If our SWA walks in asking why a certain team is getting less practice coverage than another, it's usually just seeing around a corner and seeking to avoid multiple meetings with a disgruntled sport coach. If you just listen to the admin and then calmly explain what's going, there's usually no problem.

To sum up, whenever I see a frustrated young coach, or whenever my staff sees me getting to that point, we sit down, close the office door, and go over our golden rules. We get a good laugh and then we address the issue. In my experience, life is all about reacting correctly to situations, and our golden rules have helped us do just that.

Athlete Huddle

What are some tactical ways you have solved an issue on the field/court, that can carry over into the weight room?

Coach Huddle

Do you have a rule to add to this list? What are some other ways to address tension before discussing an issue?

65

Small Moments Create Big Moments

Tim Anderson

Co-Founder - Original Strength Systems

An avalanche is full of devastating power. Capable of reaching speeds of up to 80 mph in only 5 seconds, an avalanche can change an entire landscape in a mere moment. Yet, with all that destructive power, an avalanche would never be possible without millions of tiny snowflakes. It takes unique, individual snowflakes to lay the foundation of snow that blankets a mountain. It takes an accumulation of snowflakes to eventually break away from the mountain and explode downhill. Amazing power potential lies dormant and builds snowflake by snowflake.

Just like an avalanche, the potential you possess is made possible one decision, or one action, at a time. Your success is predicated on the decisions and actions you make today. If you want to be great at something tomorrow, you must take action toward your greatness today. And just like the avalanche, through dedicated moments of action, there will be a tipping point for your success. Whether it be performance in a game, landing the job of your dreams, or having a meaningful relationship with someone you love, you can create and change the landscape of your future one moment at a time.

Athlete Huddle

Do you understand that your daily habits create your circumstances and influence your destiny?

Coach Huddle

Do your athletes see that their potential is related to their work ethic and habits? Or do they think their skills are the keys to their potential?

66

How To Be a Man

Chip Morton

Strength & Conditioning Coach - Cincinnati Bengals

After disappointing mid-season losses, we as coaches devise strategies, refine techniques, and adjust plans to get our teams back on track. In these storms, we feel frustration, discouragement, and even anger, which can sometimes spill over into flashes of temper. I had one such outburst recently in our coaches' locker room after a particularly disheartening game. I lost control of myself and uttered words I quickly regretted. Later on, after regaining my composure, I sought out one of our administrators (who'd been present during my tirade) and apologized for the remarks I'd made (even though they weren't directed at him).

The following day, I reflected on the root cause of what had occurred in the hope that I might avoid repeating it and perhaps help my staff members do the same. In my experience, we coaches tend to overuse certain words, phrases and popular anecdotes to motivate those we serve. I believe biblical stories can serve the same purpose in a fresher way.

For instance, take the Old Testament story of Gideon and the two kings of Midian. Gideon is a judge over Israel, appointed by God. His country has been overrun by the Midianites for seven years, during which several of his family members have been cruelly murdered by the invaders in a town called Tabor.

The story is pretty incredible. But to cut it way down, God raises up a mere 300 Israelite warriors through Gideon's leadership to miraculously defeat the occupying forces (120,000 strong) and reclaim their land. During the battle, Gideon takes captive both Midianite kings, Zeba and Zalmunna. After the dust has settled, he asks them who they killed in Tabor. They reply, "Men like you, each one with the bearing of a prince." Gideon then reveals that his family members were among those slain.

"As the Lord lives," Gideon says, "If you'd spared them, I would not kill you." He then instructs his son Jether to cut them down. But Jether is young and afraid.

"Come, do it yourself," the king's demand. "As is the man, so is his strength." So Gideon takes a sword and executes his prisoners.

What's the takeaway here? We're responsible for our own actions. Others may help us along the way. We may receive instruction, guidance and correction. But in the end, we are what we do. We're accountable.

As an athlete, how you study, train, practice, eat and rest will either enhance or weaken your natural abilities. You may seek advice, but the choice is always yours. The success is yours. The failure is yours. The regret is yours. Your story belongs only to you.

Athlete Huddle

Where are you failing to take ownership of your story? In what areas can you impose your will and take responsibility for your actions?

Coach Huddle

How can we come alongside our players and encourage them to bring their best attitudes and a spirit of ownership to what they're doing?

67

Investment and Ownership

Bryan Miller

Associate S&C Coach & Sports Science Coordinator - United States Naval Academy

Athletes, investing in your personal development is similar to investing in the stock market. There are always multiple and unforeseen factors that may positively or negatively influence your ROI. Needless to say, both the stock market and your daily training results are highly volatile. It's common to put a lot of money into stocks when you have the available capital, but then to forget about the investment, not checking your daily yields until something bad happens: a big loss or even bankruptcy.

This is exactly how many of you start your offseason training. You have great intentions initially, but you soon get lazy and complacent as the work becomes harder. You slack off until a wake-up call brings you back. Maybe your head coach doesn't like your effort. Maybe your teammates start passing you up. Maybe I call you out for not taking ownership of your situation.

To ensure you're staying disciplined and on track, I've placed several stock market symbols around the borders of your weekly workout sheets. They represent what you are investing in each day. In the middle of your sheet is a dollar bill. This is your ROI. Every week, the size of your return will indicate your level of success; if your efforts and training results go up, you'll earn more. If not, you won't. Either way, both you and your teammates will know exactly how hard you've trained each week and you will always be competing to obtain the most net worth. Your willingness to own your process will determine your success.

Athlete Huddle

What are the factors that positively or negatively affect your ROI?

Coach Huddle

Are you matching your players' daily investment in your program?

68

Building on the Rock

Chad Smith

Director of Strength & Conditioning - Florida International University

One story I tell my athletes is about taking your time and building a house down to the rock, the foundation. I tell this story at the beginning of either our winter training program or summer training program, usually after a challenging workout. It provides a good illustration of our why, our process. We learn and gain confidence through struggles.

I tell them we need to build our house on the rock.

There are two types of people in the world, people who spend huge amounts of money in rushing to get their houses built as quickly as possible and people who take their time, maybe even years, to build their houses properly.

The people who want their houses built right away don't care about foundations. They don't want to take time in paying attention to every detail or facing daily obstacles during construction; they hire people to expedite that process for them. Their main concern is how fast the house can be built, so they can enjoy the finished product and show it off to their peers. They want an immediate fix. They want what they want, and they don't care how many shortcuts it takes to get there. These people's homes are built on top of the ground. But they don't know that, because they didn't do the work themselves.

Then there's the other type. These people do care about foundations. It's a challenge to dig down all the way to bedrock. It takes time, patience, and a lot of hard work. But when you build a house yourself, when you face every challenge personally, you learn from those challenges personally. Every mistake you make teaches you a lesson. Every roadblock you address eliminates weakness, not just in what you're building, but in yourself, as well. You identify problems. You identify solutions. You grow. Every failure shows you how to make your house stronger. You build, mess up, tear down, and start over.

All throughout your process, those around you (who've already finished their houses) may be laughing. But you know something they don't. You know storms are coming.

Storms always come, and when they do, they test the strength of what's been built. You're not preparing your house for a sunny day. You're preparing for the storms. When the winds begin to blow, the houses built above ground will eventually fly away or collapse. But not yours. You've spent time testing the strength of every last piece. You know your house will stand because you built it on the rock. And as hard as the work was, you'll have no regrets when your house is the last one standing. You won't fear any storm.

Athlete Huddle

Which type of person are you? How can you tell?

146

Coach Huddle

How does this principle apply to your training program? How can you ensure your athletes are building their houses on the rock?

69

A Tale of Two Wolves

David Jack

Owner - Activprayer

An old Cherokee teaches his grandson about life. "A fight is going on inside me," he says to the boy. "It's between two wolves. One is evil. He represents anger, envy, sorrow, regret, greed, arrogance, guilt, resentment, inferiority, lies, false pride, superiority, and ego. The other wolf is good. He is joy, peace, love, hope, serenity, humility, kindness, benevolence, empathy, generosity, truth, compassion, and faith."

He points at his grandson. "The same battle is happening inside you and everyone else."

"Which wolf will win?" the boy asks.

The old Cherokee replies, "Whichever one you feed."

Athlete Huddle

Which wolf are you feeding?

Coach Huddle

What does this fight look like in the weight room?

70

The Other ABC - Always Be Communicating

Stuart Venable

Head Strength Coach - Lincoln North Star High School (NE)

I was running an after-school training session one afternoon when a teacher approached me and said one of our athletes (we'll call him Raymond) had mouthed off to her. She told me he'd cursed at her when she tried to engage him in conversation. Would I mind speaking to him about it? The following morning, I saw Raymond in the hall and called him into the weight room. As soon as he entered, I laid into him for showing Ms. Trent disrespect and for using profane language. He stood there, hanging his head, saying "Yes sir, yes sir." When I'd finished, I took him to Ms. Trent's office and made him apologize. She heard him out, said she forgave him and expressed that she cared about him. That's why she'd brought him snacks and paid for his lunch in the past.

When we got back to the weight room, I told Raymond that if he ever disrespected one of our staff members again, I'd permanently ban him from the weight room.

Later that day, Ms. Trent came to thank me for addressing the situation. She also shared some of Raymond's story. His mother had committed suicide on Thanksgiving Day the previous year. He'd struggled with suicidal thoughts ever since. Raymond's two older brothers were both incarcerated, one in Mississippi and one in Nebraska. He had no contact with his biological father and currently lived with his grandmother, who frequently abused him verbally.

On one hand, I felt like a schmuck for yelling at him. On the other hand, he needed to be held accountable for his actions. The bottom line was that if I or some other coach had cultivated a better relationship with Raymond, the entire situation with Ms. Trent could possibly have been avoided.

Since that day, Raymond has become a successful member of our school powerlifting team, winning numerous medals. He's progressed to the Advanced Weight Training Class and is also my Student Assistant for a beginners' class. He has a job at a restaurant and is earning his own income. Lastly, Raymond is on track to graduate this year alongside his peers and attend a community college.

Athlete Huddle

Are you keeping things bottled up inside because of fear or shame? Are you consistently communicating with your coaches about your health, wellbeing, stresses and concerns?

Coach Huddle

Does every athlete on your team have a relationship either with you or with another coach? Are you continually building your team culture by discussing goals, values, people and processes?

71

Keith Askins

Bill Foran

Strength & Conditioning Coach - Miami Heat

Here's a story I share with young athletes, especially those who haven't been drafted. It's about Keith Askins.

In 1990, after his college career had ended, Keith landed a tryout with the Miami Heat as a courtesy to his college coach, Wimp Sanderson at the University of Alabama. Keith was 6'8" and came in at 185 lbs. Yes, he was 6'8" and 185 lbs. To everyone's surprise, he outworked the other athletes in fall camp and made our team on a one-year contract through pure effort and outstanding work ethic. The next summer, he didn't miss a single workout and came into camp at 198 lbs. Despite his gains, Keith had to prove himself again. In fact, he had to prove himself on one-year contracts for five straight seasons before he got a multi-year contract.

His weight went from 185 to 198 to 208 to 215 to 220. Each summer, Keith would ask for my vacation schedule so he could take his vacation at the same time. He was so dedicated and driven that he would not miss a single workout. He became a tremendous perimeter defender and

developed a solid outside shot. He had a fine nine-year career with the Miami Heat, which at the time was an NBA record for an undrafted player.

Athlete Huddle

What can you learn from Keith's story?

Coach Huddle

How can you effectively push your athletes to follow Keith's example?

72

The Sweet Spot

Michelle Diltz

Strength & Conditioning Coach - University of Alabama

Years after I first set foot on my university's softball field, I regretted it. I don't regret my teammates (friends for life), my coaches, my degree, my life lessons or how much I grew. I regret not playing to the best of my ability because I was full of fear. I played scared. Every pitch of every out during most practices and games, I played scared. I was scared of failure and of disappointing my coaches and teammates.

But there were some instances that I remember when I played free of failure, and those times were magical. I remember the grass under my feet, the sun shining brightly and the ball hit hard to the right-center gap. I remember feeling free, just me and the softball. My eyes locked in, my legs moving swiftly, and the ball landing in my outstretched glove. I was in that sweet spot of play where you actually play because you love it. There wasn't any fear of failure during those times. There was just me loving the game.

I look back now and know that I was scared so much that I never truly played. That is my regret. I never truly played. Don't look back 10, 20 or 30 years from now and regret this wonderful time of living out your dream, playing the sport that you love. Love this time; cherish it, work hard, and live life in that sweet spot.

Athlete Huddle

What can you do to find the sweet spot? If you did play in the sweet spot, what would it look and feel like?

Coach Huddle

Are you helping your athletes play in their sweet spot? What would coaching in the sweet spot look like?

73

Tastes Great! Less Filling!

Jeff Friday

Assistant Strength & Conditioning Coach - Cincinnati Bengals

Bubba Smith, a former football star, was also famous for his Miller Lite beer commercials. In 1985, Michigan State made Bubba the grand marshal of its homecoming parade. As he rode through the student-lined streets, one side of the crowd shouted the first half of his Miller Lite catchphrase, "Tastes great!" The other side shouted back, "Less filling!"

Not long after the parade, Bubba discontinued making commercials for Miller Lite. He'd feared his sponsorship contributed to excessive alcohol consumption among students, and the parade had convinced him. The truth is, Bubba didn't drink! But when Miller had originally approached him with a large amount of money, he'd told himself that appearing in a few ads didn't mean he was compromising his principles.

Though it meant a large financial loss, Bubba ended his relationship with Miller. Why? Because he felt something much larger was at stake.

Luke 17:1 says, "Things that make people fall into sin are bound to happen, but how terrible for the one who makes them happen!" Our words and examples affect others in ways we don't always understand.

What message are you sending with your life? How are you affecting the lives of those you lead? Like physicians, coaches and athletes should keep this ancient oath in mind: "First, do no harm."

Athlete Huddle

How often do you consider the example you're setting for those who look up to you? If you could send one message with your life, what would it be? Do your actions align with it?

Coach Huddle

Are you as invested in the personal wellbeing of your athletes as you are in their physical well being?

74

Live Intentionally

Mitch Hauschildt

Prevention, Rehab & Physical Performance Coordinator

"Consistently repeated daily actions + time = inconquerable results." - Jeff Olson

In his book The Slight Edge, Jeff Olson, a highly successful business leader, observes that most respected individuals aren't successful because of major breaks, luck or gifts from others. Rather, the vast majority have accomplished great things because they consistently perform small disciplines every single day. The cumulative effect of small actions adds up over time to make a very large impact.

Unfortunately, most of us aren't disciplined enough to perform consistent daily tasks in all areas of our lives, which is why we aren't as successful as we could be in sports, school, relationships, work or our faith. But the truth is, you're list doesn't need to get any longer for you to accomplish great things. Simply commit to living every piece of your life intentionally. That means you should be tackling everything you do consciously and deliberately. Commit to having a plan and doing it well with the resources you have. When it's time to train, train hard and intelligently. When it's time to eat, fuel your body properly. When it's time to rest, block out all distractions and recover from your exertions. When it's time to enjoy friends or family, focus on that time and be present. This will bring a focus and a purpose to your life that will certainly help you achieve goals that many people may think are beyond reach.

Athlete Huddle

In what areas of your life do you find yourself going through the motions? How can you encourage your teammates to live more intentionally?

Coach Huddle

Do you regularly analyze your lifestyle and identify habits you wish were different? Do you have the power to address those habits?

75

The Extra Mile

Lorenzo Guess

Associate Head S&C Coach/Director of Player Enrichment - Michigan State University

Every day, you have a choice. When you work out or go to class, you get to decide how much effort you're going to give? Will you give a little bit? Maybe the normal amount? Will you go harder than usual? Will you go all out? Few choose that last option. Few make going all out a habit, and that offers you an advantage.

Going the extra mile isn't common. If it was, it'd be called going the normal mile. Why put in more effort than you need to? As long as you're keeping up with everyone else, who push yourself to try harder? Why do more? Obviously, this is a rhetorical question. By trying harder, you immediately stand out from everyone else. And that's what you want, isn't it? But when your alarm goes off, when you're tired, when your friends are staying out late, doing more is hard. It's not an easy choice to make.

The fact remains that the harder you push yourself, the more likely you are to succeed at whatever you're doing. By training your mind to embrace hardship, you set yourself up for a bright future. Want to be noticed? Want to be special? Want to be uncommon? Want to be a leader? Take the road less traveled. I promise: there are no traffic jams on the extra mile.

Athlete Huddle

Did you (or will you) go the extra mile today? Are you surrounding yourself with friends as committed to success as you are?

Coach Huddle

How are you pushing your athletes to invest effort into their futures on and off the field?

76

Tuning Fork

Michael Hill

Director of Sports Performance - Georgetown University

A tuning fork is a two-pronged metal device used by musicians as a tonal reference point. When struck, it vibrates, emitting a specific pitch to which instruments are tuned. If an ensemble performs music without tuning their instruments first, they risk producing dissonant sounds. The tuning fork is their North Star.

Like musical instruments, everything in nature vibrates to a specific frequency. Each human being has a unique energy to which he or she is tuned. When our surroundings produce that chord, we come alive. It's our superpower. In sports, we often overlook that. In our efforts to produce consistently efficient athletes, we frequently neglect to consider what makes them unique. I think that's because we're so busy emitting our own pitch. Coaches set the reference tone like tuning forks and athletes to their best to align themselves. That's not a bad thing.

Musicians in an orchestra don't all play the same note. If they did, the music would lack harmony. But they still need to be in tune with each other. Once tonally aligned, they can play their own parts and collaboratively make beautiful music. Similarly, when athletes tune themselves to the energy emitted by their coaches, their joined minds and intentions produce victories.

Simply put, athletes may be represented by the keys of a piano. The keyboardist is the coach. The music is the team's performance. And the composer is the unknown. That's what makes sport so beautiful.

Athlete Huddle

Have you ever had a coach you didn't feel in tune with? How important is it for your teammates to be on the same page?

Coach Huddle

How are your athletes receiving your energy? Do you have a tuning fork to which you seek to align your coaching style?

77

Do It Right, Do It Slight.
Do It Wrong, Do It Long

Mike Caro

Head Strength & Conditioning Coach -
Emory & Henry College

When I was a young athlete, I had a wrestling coach who was a legend at our small high school. He had been a wrestling coach since I could remember and coached the team long after I graduated. This coach had a way of getting right to the heart of a matter, whether he was coaching technique or giving life advice. There were many important lessons I learned from this coach, but the one saying that stuck with me throughout my life was: "Do it right, do it slight. Do it wrong, do it long." As an athlete, I always assumed he was referring to our conditioning and drills. Once I became a coach, I realized that this saying applies to competing, coaching, and life in general.

Athletes are used to hearing coaches say that if they don't do a drill or exercise correctly, they're going to keep trying until they do. But this quote means more than that. It's not about not messing up. It's about executing well. That's why I share it with my fellow coaches.

In any profession, if you mess up, you'll inevitably have to repeat the job. As a coach, the more you have to repeat when working with the same athletes, the longer the practices and training sessions seem. The athletes are making very little progress. The better you are as a coach, the less time you'll spend repeatedly correcting the same mistakes, which creates more time to mentor, lead and develop your program. The more mistakes you make, the longer each training session, day, and year of your career will feel. This also applies to your role as a family member, community member and staff member. In short, if you do things well, your time spent "working" will be slight. Take pride in what you do, develop your craft, and do it well. This will lead to more success for yourself and your athletes.

Athlete Huddle

How often do you catch yourself repeating the same mistakes? What will you do to prevent those mistakes from delaying your progress?

Coach Huddle

Are you committing yourself to doing things right or are you satisfied with repeating the same mistakes?

78

Don't Judge What You Can't See

Kurt Hester

Head Strength & Conditioning Coach - Louisiana Tech University

Like most strength coaches, I made countless mistakes early in my career. One of the most egregious and humbling involved misjudging an athlete's abilities.

Stephen Park was in ninth grade when he joined my training program at 6' and 190 lbs. He played offensive tackle, and he told me in our first interaction that his goal was to play college football. Stephen's size and athletic ability weren't very impressive. In my mind, I immediately discounted his ambition. Even though he showed drive and a love for lifting, he had horrible motor skills, as well as inferior quickness and mobility. As a sophomore, he grew to 6'1" and 220 lbs. He started on the junior varsity team. He improved in strength and size, but he still had Frankenstein feet and mobility issues. Nevertheless, his dream remained intact. And though I still didn't see any hope for him, I encouraged him to keep working. Between Stephen's sophomore and junior years, he grew to 6'3" and 270 lbs. He also started at offensive tackle on his varsity team and became their most dominant and violent lineman.

Even though I loved this kid as a person and a player, I still doubted his ability to play at the next level. His senior year he measured in at 6'3" and 300 lbs. That year, Stephen made first team all-district. Even though he lacked quick feet, he was one of the most dominant run blockers in the state and received offers from a couple of FCS schools in Louisiana. He chose to walk-on at Arkansas. Still being an unbeliever in his abilities, I begged him to take a full scholarship and thought it was unwise for him to pass up good offers to walk on at a school that didn't want him. But Stephen followed his dream. His grandfather's alma mater was Arkansas, so that's where he went. After his redshirt freshman year, he earned a full scholarship and a starting guard position for the next three years. He became 2nd team All-SEC and a Sporting News All-American his senior year. After that, I trained him for his pro-day and he signed a free agent contract with the Miami Dolphins.

I passed judgment on Stephen far too early in his athletic career, but I was lucky enough not to discourage him from working toward his dream. His heart and desire trumped his Frankenstein feet and my blindness.

Athlete Huddle

When have you judged one of your teammates without fully understanding his/her situation?

Coach Huddle

When we doubt a player's potential, how do we proceed? Do we believe in him? Do we encourage him? Or do we subconsciously write off their success?

79

Be Careful What You Plant

Anthony Morando

Manager of Human Performance - Altru Health System/EXOS

Life is more predictable than many people think. It's a matter of planting seeds and tending crops. If you plant honesty, you will reap trust. If you plant goodness, you will reap friends. If you plant humility, you will reap greatness. If you plant perseverance, you will reap victory. If you plant consideration, you will reap harmony. If you plant hard work, you will reap success. If you plant forgiveness, you will reap reconciliation. If you plant openness, you will reap intimacy. If you plant patience, you will reap improvement. If you plant faith, you will reap miracles.

On the other hand, if you plant dishonesty, you will reap distrust. If you plant selfishness, you will reap loneliness. If you plant pride, you will reap destruction. If you plant envy, you will reap trouble. If you plant laziness, you will reap stagnation. If you plant bitterness, you will reap isolation. If you plant greed, you will reap loss. If you plant gossip, you will reap enemies. If you plant worry, you will reap wrinkles. If you plant sin,

you will reap guilt.

You will be dealt with as you deal with others. You will reap what you sow. Be careful what you plant now, because it will determine what you harvest tomorrow.

Athlete Huddle

What seeds are you planting?

Coach Huddle

What does your ideal harvest look like? Have you stopped to consider if you're planting the right seeds?

80

Small Details Make Large Impacts

Matt Shaw

Director of Sports Performance - University of Denver

Imagine trying to solve a very complex puzzle made up of small, intricate pieces.

You begin with the obvious parts, like the puzzle's edges. They're usually pretty easy to piece together, and they provide a kind of framework for everything else. But then things become more challenging. You group together pieces that resemble each other. You do your best to organize your workflow. However, as you progress from one stage to the next, assembling the puzzle demands increased focus, patience and diligence. Even the smallest of mistakes can cause confusion and substantial delay. But piece by piece, the larger image grows plain. And when you're done, you enjoy stepping back to admire what you've accomplished.

Achieving success is a complicated process that requires persistence and the ability to learn from your mistakes. Sometimes the greatest lessons are learned through frustration and multiple attempts. The point is that every little detail of how you discipline yourself, train and manage your lifestyle impacts the final result. Those who focus on the little things and diligently work to achieve small gains end up accomplishing great feats in the long run than those who don't. Never say something is too small to matter. Everything matters, because in the end, your big picture is only as good as the small puzzle pieces of which it's made.

Athlete Huddle

Identify a goal (a championship, a PR, etc.). What is one habit you could implement that would improve the odds of you achieving that goal?

Coach Huddle

Identify a moment in your life that you succeeded in something after multiple failed attempts. What did that process look like? What ultimately made the difference between success and failure?

81

The Farmer and the Mule

Scott Bennett

Assistant Athletic Director for Sports Performance - Radford University

Afarmer had an old mule that fell into a deep, dry well and began to cry loudly. Looking down at the trapped animal, he mopped his forehead and considered how difficult, nigh impossible, it would be to rescue it. Because the mule was old and the well was dry, the farmer fetched his shovel, planning to bury the animal in the well.

He called upon his neighbors to help him and they agreed. To work they went. Mounds of dirt began to fall on the mule's back. He became hysterical. But then, the mule did something unexpected. Each time they would throw a shovelful of dirt on his back, he would shake it off and pack it down, raising himself up, inch by inch. Shovelful after shovelful, the mule would shake it off and step up. Exhausted and dirty, but quite alive, the mule eventually stepped over the top of the well and walked through the crowd.

This is a story I tell our kids when adversity strikes. Even though you may feel like you can't overcome the problem in front of you, even though you may feel like there's no way out, there is always an answer. Shake it off and step up. The load you carry may feel overwhelming, but if you can shake it off, one shovelful at a time, and step up, one step at a time, there is no amount of adversity you can't overcome.

Athlete Huddle

Are you ready to quit?

Coach Huddle

When facing adversity, how can keep the "big picture" in view and get the student-athletes over their first hurdle in the process of defeating adversity?

82

Being Proactive, Not Reactive

Marty Barnett

Director of Strength & Conditioning - Rejoice Christian School (OK)

"Now there were some terrible seeds on the planet that was the home of the little prince, and these were the seeds of the baobab. The soil of that planet was infested with them. A baobab is something you will never, never be able to get rid of if you attend to it too late. It spreads over the entire planet. It bores clear through it with its roots. And if the planet is too small, and the baobabs are too many, they split it into pieces…"

As the narrator in The Little Prince discovered, being proactive is vital to "weeding" out the bad. Or as the great philosopher Barney Fife would say, "Nip it in the bud!" The Little Prince had to take action, or the bad seeds would grow into enormous Baobab trees that would overtake and kill his little planet. Staying proactive in the removal of bad plants was vital. The Baobabs in the story of the Little Prince are a metaphor for small habits, behaviors, and attitudes in our lives. If left to grow, they can overtake us and destroy our goals, relationships, etc. The little things matter. We must guard against this. Nip it! Practice good habits, good effort, good attitudes, good technique.

"'It is a question of discipline,' the little prince said to me later on…'You must see to it that you pull up regularly all the baobabs, at the very first moment when they can be distinguished from the rose bushes which they resemble so closely in their earliest youth. It is very tedious work,' the little prince added, 'but very easy.'"

Waiting to pull up the baobabs can have disastrous consequences. At the very least, it can impede your progress or keep you from your goals. Prepare with purpose every day. Just as uprooting the bad seeds is important, sowing good seeds is as well. We want the fruit of our labor and the fruit of our character to be good and pleasing. The Bible says in Matthew 12:33-34, "Make a tree good and its fruit will be good, or make a tree bad and its fruit will be bad, for a tree is recognized by its fruit. You brood of vipers, how can you who are evil say anything good? For the mouth speaks what the heart is full of."

Athlete Huddle

Are your habits and attitudes going to help you achieve your goals? What behaviors do you need to nip?

Coach Huddle

Are you recognizing bad habits and attitudes in your life? What are you doing to uproot them? How can you speak into your athletes to encourage good habits and attitudes?

83

Kill the Cow

Stu Roche

Assistant Director of Sports Performance - Marquette University

A monk and his young pupil were traveling a desolate road. The sun was about to set, so the monk ordered his pupil to run on ahead and seek lodging. The lad did as he was instructed and soon came upon a lonely hovel by the roadside. He knocked on the door and asked if he and his master might rest there until morning. The small family inside agreed and prepared a humble meal of milk and cheese for their visitors.

During dinner, the young student posed a question to his hosts. "If you don't mind me asking, how do you survive here in the middle of nowhere?" The wife looked to her husband for a response. He gave one.

"We have a cow," he said. "We sell its milk to our neighbor, who lives nearby. We keep back enough for ourselves to drink and make some cheese. That's how we live."

The student pondered the family's poverty until late that night, touched by their humility and simple generosity. The following morning, the travelers continued their journey. Before they had gone far, the monk addressed his pupil. "Go back and kill the cow," he said. His student was dumbfounded. Kill the cow?

"Master, that cow is all they have. If it dies, they die! Please reconsider."

The monk did not yield. "Kill the cow," he insisted. "Push it off a cliff." The youth was heartbroken, but his vow of obedience obligated him to follow orders. He did as he was told.

Years later, the boy grew to be a monk himself and found himself traveling the same lonely road, this time alone. As he rounded a familiar bend, a splendid mansion came into view exactly where the hovel had sat years earlier. Perplexed, he again knocked on the door. A gentleman answered in fine clothes.

"Where is the family that used to live here?"

The man looked confused. "My family and I have always lived here," he replied.

"No," the young monk persisted. "I stayed with a poor family in their hut on this exact spot when I was young. Where are they?"

"Ah, we used to live in a hut," the gentleman continued. "But one day, our cow fell to its death and we were forced to find other means of livelihood. That was a difficult time. But the challenge helped us identify other skills and resources that lay at our disposal. We're now much better off than before."

Athlete Huddle

What do you think the young man would have seen as he rounded that bend the second time if he'd not killed the cow?

Coach Huddle

What do you think the cow represents? Do you know of any cows that need to be killed?

84

Echo Mountain

Rick Court

NCAA Strength & Conditioning Coach

A son and his father were walking in the mountains. Suddenly, the son fell, hurt himself and screamed in pain. To his surprise, he heard his cries repeated a little way off. Curious, he yelled, "Who are you?" The echo responded, "Who are you?" He cried again, "I'm the best!" The echo responded, "I'm the best!"

Angered at the response, he cried, "Coward!" He received the answer, "Coward!" He looked to his father and asked, "What's going on?"

The father smiled and said, "My son, pay attention." Then he hollered, "You are a champion!" The father's echo responded, "You are a champion!" The son didn't understand. His father explained, "People call this an echo. But really, this is life. It gives you back everything you say or do. Life is simply a reflection of our actions. If you want more love in the world, create more love in your heart. If you want more competence in your team, improve your competence. This relationship applies to everything, in all aspects of life. Life will give you back everything you give away. Your life is not a coincidence. It's a reflection of you."

Athlete Huddle

Think of a time when the "echo" was not what you wanted to hear. Did you do something to try and change it? What did you do?

Coach Huddle

Do your actions reflect your goals? Do you share experiences with your players and teach them to walk the path toward a great reflection?

85

Commitment

Jerry Palmieri

34 Year Veteran NFL/NCAA S&C Coach - Super Bowl Champion XLII and XLVI

A chicken and a pig are having breakfast together. Their waitress comes over to take their order. Chicken pipes up, "We'll have bacon and eggs!" But the pig objects.

"Hold on there! That meal only requires partial commitment from you. It requires full commitment from me!"

How committed are you to training, to competing, to your team, to your family, to your faith? Under certain circumstances, would you sell out? Or are you all in, prepared to give everything you have toward achieving your goals? You can't determine the skills you're born with. You can't determine a lot of things. But you can always control the amount of effort you bring to what you do.

John Wooden said, "We don't have to be superstars. All we have to do is learn to rise to every occasion, give our best effort, and make those around us better as we do so." Never leave the field, gym, court, mat, track, or weight room knowing you could have given more.

It comes down to your attitude. The way you react to difficulty tells your story. A negative attitude will hold you back; a positive attitude opens the door to your fullest potential. Let your life shine with a victorious light! How committed are you to being great? Champions give all they have.

Athlete Huddle

Are you the chicken or the pig?

Coach Huddle

Coach, when the new year comes, do you reevaluate your training cycle and make appropriate upgrades or do you simply change the dates on the previous year's program?

86

Words for Achieving Goals in Life and Sport

Evan Simon

Head Strength & Conditioning Coach - Davidson College

W hat follows is a collection of words that I share with the student-athletes I'm fortunate to work with daily. If you live out the meanings of these words every day, you'll have a team of hard-working, tough, mature individuals capable of achieving great things. Moreover, these words hold the potential to transform not only your success in sport but also in life.

1. Details

Understand exactly what is expected of you, what needs to get done. Fully comprehending the role you play is key to success.

2. Determination

Apply a sense of purpose to your task. Apply your will. What would you give up to achieve your goal? Determination means demonstrating your commitment to what you're doing.

3. Effort

Effort is your determined attempt at something you're aiming for. It involves strenuous physical and mental exertion. And it's always fully under your control. Are you looking to succeed? Start here.

4. Accountability

Be responsible and accountable for your actions. Maturity means receiving instruction and understanding a situation through another's eyes. Taking criticism empowers you to learn from your mistakes. It requires humility and a lot of vulnerability. But it can transform your approach to life, as well as your success in sport.

5. Family

A family is a collection of people bound together by common goals and affiliations. As a member of a team, structured pursuit of success pulls you closer to those around you. There aren't many opportunities in life to be involved in something that can provide so much camaraderie, intimacy, vulnerability, and friendship. Value that process. Value what it creates.

Athlete Huddle

Which of these words stuck out to you? How might you modify their definitions to suit your specific situation?

Coach Huddle

How can you as a member of this staff provide further insight into the value of these principles for your athletes? How can you leverage these concepts to help them grow?

87

Remember This

Matt Jennings

Head Strength & Conditioning Coach - Xavier University

One of my favorite quotes comes from Elbert Hubbard:

"If you work for a man, in heaven's name work for him, speak well of him, and stand by the institution he represents. Remember, an ounce of loyalty is worth a pound of cleverness. If you must growl, condemn, and eternally find fault - resign your position, and when you are outside, damn to your heart's content - but as long as you are part of the institution, do not condemn it. If you do, the first high wind that comes along will blow you away, and probably you will never know why."

Many coaches chase logos. Many poke holes in the techniques of others. Many allow their egos to supersede their callings. Let us remember that coaching means serving. And as Hubbard notes, "an ounce of loyalty is worth a pound of cleverness." Be present in your position. Be passionate. Seek to build up those around you.

Athlete Huddle

Describe one of the most memorable demonstrations of loyalty that you've witnessed. How do you define the perfect team player?

Coach Huddle

Anyone can tell a story or offer a pep talk. But how do you build loyalty in a group of athletes?

88

Dancing in the Rain

Michelle Diltz

Strength & Conditioning Coach - University of Alabama

The rain continued to fall at an annoying rate (not really sprinkling, not really down pouring either), but the game continued. The game was not just any game. It was the third game in the Women's College World Series Championship in which the winner took all. The game was approaching midnight after hours of rain delays.

Both teams had put in the work throughout their season with hours of softball practice and strength and conditioning to get to this point, but the home team was in the lead. The momentum was changing though and the visitors in the dugout weren't worried about the rain because they were stringing together some timely hits. As the rain continued to fall, the home team's attitude started falling with every complaint they made.

The umpire called a rain delay. Both teams went to their dugouts, and I'm convinced that what happened next shifted the outcome of the game. The home team went to their dugout, put their jackets on, sat down on the benches and looked miserable while the visiting team chose to stand together to dance in the rain. They had a grand old time.

In the end, the best softball players did not win, but the best softball team did. Playing for each other by controlling what they could control, their attitude and their effort, they claimed their victory. They rode their fun and excitement all the way to the end, celebrating by dancing in the rain.

Athlete Huddle

Do you sit and pout when things aren't going your way or do you dance in the rain? What are some things you can't control that affect your play? How can you make changes to your attitude and effort?

Coach Huddle

Can you prepare your athletes to dance in the rain instead of pouting in the dugout? What are some things that you can change when coaching to focus on effort and attitude?

89

All In

Dan Noble

Director of Athlete Performance - The Hill Academy

"All In" is a common phrase in sports these days. It usually ends up on the back of a t-shirt or in a memorable pre-game speech. People feel drawn to it because it's simple, punchy, and does a good job of evoking the kind of big success that can be achieved by a team of selfless, passionate, dedicated individuals working together toward a single goal. It's a powerful phrase because it pumps you up and offers belief in what you're able to accomplish if you pour all of your force into what you're doing.

I must say, as I've spent the last eleven years coaching hundreds of athletes on various levels, I've seen "All In" lose some of its potency. Day to day, I'll ask my athletes, "What's your goal?" They'll usually respond that they want to play Division 1 or go pro. Then I'll ask if they're all in on that goal. The response is always the same.

"Yes, sir!"

Then I'll ask them what they ate for breakfast that morning. When did they go to sleep last night? Did they give their absolute best in the gym today? Do their friend groups reflect their goals? What do they spend their time doing off the field? Which of their habits sets them apart from thousands of other kids competing for the same goal? What are they doing to improve their worst subject? It's around this time they usually start to regret having the conversation with me.

Too many people these days confuse movement with progress. They think that just because they practice every day and carry a protein shake around, they're all in. But at the next level, those things are taken for granted. Those things are the bare minimum. Everyone trains, fuels, and practices. I'll ask my athletes a second time what their goals are. And this time, I'll typically get the same responses, but with less enthusiasm.

That's when I explain that I'm not trying to crush their dreams, but rather to get them on the actual path to achieving them. Does breakfast really matter? Do friends really matter? Do academics matter? Everything matters. And if you're serious about landing a career that few people ever get to have, every aspect of your life needs to support that intention.

I tell my athletes to go home and write their goals in their journals. "Then evaluate your life to see if all of your habits align with your desired outcome." Are they truly all in? What would it look like to be actually all in on your dream? Big goals require big sacrifices. And when it comes down to it, most athletes have no idea how much work is actually involved. They're in love with the dream, but unwilling to accept the hardships that come along with it.

Athlete Huddle

Do your habits support your goals? Does your work ethic demonstrate just how badly you want to succeed?

Coach Huddle

Are you just showing up to the weight room, or are you daily working as hard as you can to push your athletes towards the goals they've expressed?

90

Nothing But Time

Blair Wagner

Owner & CEO - DIA Sports Performance

T ime is a peculiar thing. Sometimes we wish it would hustle by. Sometimes we wish it would freeze on command. We can't buy it, trade it, or save it. And we don't get any more or less of it than any of the teams we face. It's neutral. Each team has the same amount. And once it's gone, there's no getting it back. These moments are precious.

Each day, you get to choose how you'll spend your time. Not if, only how. Use it or lose it, the hours tick by. Time is so easy to waste. It's so easy to let the minutes slip away into aimless pursuits that don't influence the big picture. And time never forgives. It doesn't care if you take it for granted. It won't apologize if it runs out before you're ready. You can invest thousands of moments in a hard-earned win and never regret the sacrifice. Or you can let time become your worst enemy.

Fight to make every minute count. Fight to invest each second in the success of your team. Hold yourself accountable. Hold each other accountable. Remember our why. Only two things matter: our team and our mission. Time only offers so many opportunities. Enjoy them. Take advantage of them. Because when they're gone, memories are the only things remaining. What kinds of memories are we going to build today?

Athlete Huddle

What separates us from the rest of the teams we will face this year?

Coach Huddle

What's one thing we want to be remembered for?

91

Breaking Boulders

Grant Geib

Director of Football Strength & Conditioning - Western Michigan University

S
port teaches us to embrace challenges. However, we've all encountered situations in which the challenges ahead seem more like roadblocks. There is no clear path to victory. In these situations, our will, resolve, and perseverance are tested to their limits. How do we fight through these

challenges?

A catastrophic rockslide once struck a medieval kingdom. The rubble was cleared over time, except for one giant boulder that blocked the road to the castle. It was too heavy to move, so people resigned themselves to walking around it. That is, everyone except for a stubborn soldier. He'd spent years helping to build the road. He took pride in his work. He determined to somehow move the boulder, so he took a hammer in his hand and began swinging on the obstruction. Hour after hour, day after day he persevered. The boulder remained unfazed. Weeks went by, and the youth's ambition began to fade.

He'd just about lost hope when one day, an old man happened by and offered to lend a hand. The young soldier explained that he'd already hit the boulder a thousand times, that he was about to give up. But the old man took the hammer, drew a deep breath and shattered the rock with a single swing.

The soldier shook his head in disbelief. He demanded to know the old man's secret. Smiling, the gentleman said, "It wasn't a single blow that broke the rock. It was the thousand that came before it."

Perseverance is one of the greatest attributes an athlete can have. Countless hours of training and preparation go into every competition, and there will always be moments when your determination is tested. Is it worth it? Will the hard work pay off? It will, and despite the grueling journey, the truth is that the effort on the front end often determines the outcome on game day. For this reason, we need to trust the process and approach challenges one swing at a time. When that breakthrough finally occurs, take pride in the thousands of swings that made it happen, and enjoy knowing that you earned your success.

Athlete Huddle

Do you go around the boulder or try to break it? What motivates you to fight through life's challenges? What is your why?

Coach Huddle

What are some "boulders" you've faced in your life or coaching career? How did you overcome them?

92

Look Within

Joe Quinlin

Director of Strength & Conditioning - Northwest Missouri State University

W hen I started at Northwest Missouri State University as Head Strength and Conditioning Coach, their football program had been to three consecutive national championship games. As the only new addition to their coaching staff, I felt a lot of pressure to succeed and subsequently focused all of my attention on outworking the teams that had defeated us in previous years. Whatever they were doing, I was determined to go farther, longer and harder.

Now as I look back on that time, I realize I'd given myself an impossible task. Every team is unique and every year is unique. Nonetheless, we dug our heels in and played another great season, landing in the championship game, which we once again lost. That's when my mindset shifted. I'd been spending so much time obsessing over rival programs, and I finally realized that I should've been focusing instead on our own unique team, on what we could actually control.

Introspection is a powerful tool. It's easy to look around and waste time observing other teams. But choosing to focus instead on improving on your own is the first step to success.

Are we better than we were yesterday, a week ago, a year ago? If not, why? To whom are we accountable? What's our plan for addressing the weaknesses we've identified in ourselves? The answers vary, depending on the person. Some bring energy every day. Others require regular prodding. But we must all share in the unified intention to continually improve. That's culture.

So we decided to turn over our training sessions to the upperclassmen. As a staff, we'd still be on hand to lead groups and provide cues when needed. But the leadership largely came from our athletes themselves. I believe that made a huge impact. It helped them view training through a different lens. Why? Because nobody can hand you success. It never comes from the outside. It's born within and grows as each team member discovers and nurtures it.

Athlete Huddle

Are you evaluating your personal growth daily, weekly, monthly, yearly?

Coach Huddle

How do you define success? What steps will you take to achieve it?

93

Aggregation of Marginal Gains

Teena Murray

Senior Director of Athlete Health & Performance - Sacramento Kings

I t's easy to dream and make goals. It's also easy to think showing up and working hard will get you those outcomes. The problem is, purpose without process doesn't get you very far.

In 2010, Dave Brailsford became the new Performance Director for Team Sky (Great Britain's professional cycling team). No British cyclist had ever won the Tour de France. Brailsford's goal was to change that.

His approach was simple. Brailsford believed in a concept he called "Aggregation of Marginal Gains." He believed that if he could improve every area related to cycling performance by just one percent, the sum of those small gains would add up to significant improvement over time. He was right. His athletes started optimizing everything, from nutrition and training to the ergonomics of their bike seats and tire pressure, to the pillows they slept on, to the way they washed their hands to avoid infection. They searched for one percent improvements everywhere.

Brailsford anticipated that if they could successfully execute this strategy, Team Sky would be in a position to win the Tour de France in five years. This time he was wrong. They won it in three. Then, at the 2012

Olympic Games, they dominated, winning 70 percent of the gold medals available. In fact, many have called British cycling feats over the past decade the most successful run in modern cycling history.

What can we learn from Team Sky? First, Brailsford had a very clear goal or purpose. He wanted to win the Tour de France. He also had a very clear timeline: to win in 5 years. Most importantly, he had a very clear process. In life and in sport, identifying purpose is the easy part. Defining and committing to the process is the challenge.

It's easy to underestimate the value of small choices or better decisions. Improving by just one percent isn't notable or even noticeable. But, in the long run, it is the only way to make meaningful and lasting progress. According to Brailsford's' Aggregation of Marginal Gains, there is no difference between making a choice that is one percent better or one percent worse on the first day. But, as time unfolds, small improvements compound, creating a very big splash in the performance outcome.

Athlete Huddle

How can you be one percent better today?

Coach Huddle

How can you reframe training for your athletes to reinforce the importance of small gains?

94

The Tiny Spark

Jim Malone

Head Strength & Conditioning Coach - Pittsburgh Pirates

"**C**onsider ships... Although they are so large and are driven by strong winds, they are steered by a very small rudder wherever the pilot is inclined. In the same way, the tongue is a small part of the body but it boasts of great things... Consider how a small spark sets a great forest on fire..." (James 3)

I'm not a religious man, but these verses are interesting. They provide a great reminder of the impact, both positive and negative, that our words can have. We are charged to teach and motivate our athletes, to be aware of the power our words carry. Is the spark we're sending good or bad? Does it build up or tear down? This applies to other conversations, as well, whether with colleagues, family members, even strangers.

It's important to get to know the players under your care, to understand what motivates them, and to dial in what kind of verbal criticism they respond best to. Maybe they need constant encouragement, or maybe they're resilient enough to be challenged. I've found that the athletes who've struggled more with poor behavior and self-discipline are the ones who have been barraged with negativity. They usually respond to a more positive approach.

Words have immense power. We should always keep that truth in front of us and seek to let our words be the tiny spark that becomes a raging fire of success.

Athlete Huddle

How could you better leverage the power of your words with your teammates?

Coach Huddle

How intentional are you with the words you use? When was the last time you said something to an athlete that you could tell made an immediate impact?

95

Difficulty

Eric Overland

Supervisor of Strength & Conditioning - Wayne State University

I believe that if you employ a positive attitude, your greatest challenges and hardships can turn into your most satisfying joys and successes. The problem is, that attitude isn't so easy to maintain, especially when the process of achieving your desired outcome ends up taking longer than you expected. We're used to quick fixes. But the truth is, hard work sometimes takes a while to pay off. And in this world of streamed entertainment and next-day delivery, that can require more patience than many people are willing to give.

I think coaches and athletes may have a better perspective on this than most other people. Think about it. We train for competition. We identify weaknesses and we work to correct them. That takes time and effort. But on game day (whether a week, a month, or two years later), we get to observe the direct effects of our labors.

Every year, we get a new batch of incoming freshmen. Now that strength and conditioning has more of a foothold in high schools than it used to, the situation's improved. But we still encounter a lot of bad habits in those kids. The two most common issues we see are weak posterior chains and what I call weak point-A-to-point-B technique. For example, an athlete may have been taught to squat by being told to sit down and stand up. No specific cues or techniques were offered which may have helped him do so correctly and safely.

I'll tell you what. Breaking those habits takes time. Let's say an incoming athlete has been training consistently for four years. That means we may have to correct four years of bad training. I'm not saying it will take that long, but moving forward sometimes requires taking a step back, which means hard work and patience. The great thing about difficulty is that we usually can't overcome it on our own. We're forced to reach out for help. It takes humility and vulnerability to let someone else into your problem, but that's the only way forward. And in the process of addressing your hardship, you'll most likely develop a relationship with whoever helped you. That's the gift adversity gives us. It can melt us down, but as we recover, we create bonds with those around us.

The problem is, we still do our best to avoid difficulty. Even though we see the victories of those who come through the fire, we're disinclined to feel the heat ourselves. That's a mental game. Understand that your greatest chance of success requires jumping into the fire and leaning on those around you for support. It will make you better, and it offers relationship that truly can't be forged any other way.

Athlete Huddle

Do you ever see your teammates struggling in ways that you've struggled? How could you demonstrate more transparency about the struggles you've experienced?

Coach Huddle

How can you model the humility and willingness to share personal burdens that you'd like to see in your athletes?

96

The Wall

Matt Johnson

Director of Men's Basketball Strength & Conditioning - Butler University

Over 58,000 young American soldiers died during the Vietnam War. We honor them with a memorial of etched marble in the shape of a healing wound just a few blocks from our campus. It reminds us what freedom costs.

Many coaches throw around the word "sacrifice." But I've found that most kids don't fully understand what it means. Sometimes drawing a parallel helps.

Every athlete has a dream. They want to excel in their sports. They want to go pro. They enlist to accomplish that goal.

Soldiers also have dreams. Many want to become doctors or lawyers, start businesses, get married and raise children, etc. When they get deployed, they put those dreams on the back burner so we can pursue ours.

My dad was on a UDT (Underwater Demolition Team), the predecessor of the Seal team. I grew up hearing his stories, looking at his military scrapbooks. Each face was a story, and they all ended the same: "He was killed in action." I couldn't see the parallel when I was young, but I do now. Sacrifice means putting your goals aside so others can accomplish theirs.

Every Wednesday during summer training camp, our men's basketball team visits The Wall. They pay homage to our fallen heroes, and each player remembers a name. We hang those soldiers' profiles in our weight room for the remainder of the summer. By the time school starts, that wall is full, and it serves as a reminder of what sacrifice means.

Our kids have transformed, and none more than a freshman this past year who said, "If they can take a bullet for us, then a few jumping jacks and push-ups aren't really that hard." Athletes need to sacrifice to achieve their goals. But first, they need to understand what sacrifice means. Our act of remembrance and respect has changed our athletes mentally and physically. It will forever be the centerpiece of our offseason training.

Athlete Huddle

Every day you get to work toward your dreams. Are you grateful for that opportunity?

Coach Huddle

The sets and reps will eventually fade. What are you doing today to be remembered as a mentor?

97

Sharpen the Axe!

Dave Abernathy

Co-Founder/Director of Education & Sales - Tsunami Bar/Total Strength & Speed

G rowing up on a farm, I got very familiar with various types of machinery and tools. I learned very quickly that if your tools are not in top working order, it makes your job that much harder. Before beginning any good work, it's always better to take some time and ensure maintenance, safety and efficiency are present and accounted for. Abraham Lincoln stated, "Give me six hours to chop down a tree and I will spend the first four sharpening the axe." Ecclesiastes 10:10 says, "Using a dull axe requires great strength, so sharpen the blade. That's the value of wisdom: it helps you succeed." Making our players faster, stronger and more powerful has always been a worthy goal, but let's not forget to sharpen the axe! The sharper the axe, the easier it is to get the job done. Big, fast and strong are great, but players execute most effectively when they are sharp.

On the farm, my dad and grandfather used a whetstone, an abrasive stone that sharpens knives, hatchets and axes. Our challenge as strength coaches is to be that whetstone for our athletes. I try to always tell my players the truth. Sometimes the truth may seem negative, but a hard truth is better than an easy lie. Think of charging a car battery. It can't be done without a negative and positive charge. Be that abrasive whetstone that sharpens the axe, and be the smooth cloth that cleans the blade. Constructive feedback followed by affirmation and encouragement.

How do you apply this in the weight room? Simple. Love your players as your own. Their job is to love each other and your job is to love them. You can't just be a great motivator; you have to be a great teacher, too. Model the way and walk the talk. These lessons can be easy to preach but hard to live out. When you face adversity, your athletes are studying the way you respond. Players follow those they trust, so lay a path that will help them most effectively execute their plan and reach their desired destination.

Athlete Huddle

What does it mean to be sharp? How can you ensure your blade stays sharpened?

Coach Huddle

What is the most efficient way to promote "sharpness" in your athletes? Who are they taking cues from?

98

Bad Days

Sam Gardner

Sport Physiologist: Strength & Conditioning - United States Olympic Committee

Someone once said, "There are people who would love to have your bad days." Think about that for a second. Have you had a bad day recently? I know I have. I recently tore a ligament. I remember hobbling around at

work when an athlete I was training asked me what was wrong. I began complaining about the soreness. In that moment, I became focused solely on my own discomfort. The athlete responded, "It must be nice to feel your knee." You see, he'd been paralyzed in a car accident years earlier and could no longer move his legs. But instead of feeling sorry for himself, he'd learned to play wheelchair tennis. He'd also gone on to win medals in four Paralympic Games, as well as more Grand Slams than any other male athlete in U. S. history.

I was never paralyzed in a car accident. I never woke up one day without vision, unable to see my mother when I called to her for help. I never lost my leg while serving my nation in battle. I never endured any of these "bad days" experienced by U. S. Paralympic athletes. Instead of making excuses, these inspiring individuals chose to move forward, growing stronger as a result of their hardships.

Athlete Huddle

When was the last time you made an excuse? What do you consider your disadvantages? How you could leverage those challenges to grow stronger?

Coach Huddle

Do you ever get so focused on a negative situation that you lose sight of how fortunate you are? Can you list three things for which you're grateful?

99

Balance

Zach Mathers

Director of Strength & Conditioning/Head Athletic Trainer - University of Sioux Falls

Brian Dyson, CEO of Coca-Cola, describes life as a game in which you're juggling five balls. One represents work. One is for family. The others are your health, your friends and your spirit. As you're juggling, you're doing your best to keep all five balls in the air, right? But chances are, at some point, one or more of the balls will fall. And that's when you learn what they're made of. The ball that represents work is rubber. It bounces back. But the other balls are made of glass. Dropping one of them costs you way more. If you're lucky, they only get scratched or scuffed. But glass balls can shatter. How important is your family? What about your health?

Balance is key to success. Don't take anything for granted, and be careful with the blessings you've been given. They're not unbreakable.

Athlete Huddle

How do you balance your sport with your personal life?

Coach Huddle

Have you ever made a list of life priorities? Which of these balls have you been reckless with in the past? Is true balance even possible?

100

Matt Durant

Power of Leadership

Director of Strength & Conditioning - University of La Verne

There's a story I like to recycle a lot. It's from the book Extreme Ownership by Jocko Willink and Leif Babin. During Basic Underwater Demolition/SEAL (BUD/S) training, there were six boat teams out doing PT. Each team had 6-8 members. Team no. 1 was winning everything and team no. 6 was last on each race. In BUD/S, if you win the race, you don't have the punishment of extra PT.

What the instructors saw was that Boat 1 had all the energy. They were encouraging each other and using positive reinforcement to talk to each other. Boat 6 had bad body language and they were all bickering with each other, arguing during the race. So, the instructors decided to switch Boat 1's and Boat 6's captains. Within a few races, Boat 6 was getting close to winning and Boat 1 started to slip down to the bottom. Eventually, Boat 6 started winning races and Boat 1 was dead last. All of this was due to changing the boats' leaders.

Athlete Huddle

When have you seen the power of leadership demonstrated? How have you seen good and bad leadership affect teams you've been part of?

Coach Huddle

Do you realize the importance of leadership and are you taking your role seriously? Do you understand how your leadership has a profound effect on your team's winning and losing?

102

Running on Fumes

Tanna Burge

Assistant Athletics Director Sports Performance - Texas A&M University

W hen you are running really low on gas, and then running on fumes, you get anxious. Am I going to make it to the gas station? What if I don't make it? When you finally do spot a gas station, you pull into your spot, shut off your engine, and pause while you fill up. And when you're done, you turn the ignition and watch the needle jump from empty to full.

Sometimes, we let ourselves get so run down and exhausted. Literally, we're running on fumes. It's only when we take a step back, get away from all the distractions, and pause long enough that we can reflect on where we are mentally, physically, emotionally, and spiritually. If you pause long enough and allow yourself to be filled back up, whether in the form of identity, energy, joy, peace, healing, or hope for the future, you will find renewed strength and an unhindered focus on your pursuit of greatness.

Athlete Huddle

How can you disconnect, even for a short time, to allow yourself to be filled back up? Who do you look to as a good example of someone who keeps their "tank" at appropriate levels regularly?

Coach Huddle

When do you see yourself or your athletes running on fumes the most? How can you prepare in advance so you don't hit empty?

103

How Much Water Can a Penny Hold?

Mitch Hauschildt

Prevention, Rehab & Physical Performance Coordinator - Missouri State University

How much water can a penny hold? It's kind of a strange question, I know. After all, pennies are flat, right? So they can't really hold any. Try this.

Lay a penny on a flat surface. Fill an eyedropper and start dripping water onto the coin's surface. If you're like most people, you probably assume that after the third or fourth drop, the water will start to spill over the edges. But you'd be wrong. As more water is added, a dome develops on the penny. It will continue to expand until the weight of the water becomes too much for the surface tension to control. This usually occurs after twelve or more drops. though some experiments have shown that a penny can hold as many as fifty drops before spilling.

The practical application of this activity is that we are capable of far more than we realize. When we are presented with a large, audacious goal or obstacle, most of us choose to play it safe, dialing things back to make sure we can succeed. That's because we often underestimate what we are really capable of. Why not push the limit? Why not see how far we can climb? This is an especially valuable proposition in team sports, where we commit to sticking together as a cohesive unit. When athletes and teams stick together and are willing to pursue goals that many consider impossible, unexpected things happen.

Athlete Huddle

In what areas of your life are you setting the bar too low? Do you have audacious goals? Does aiming to high scare you? Why?

Coach Huddle

How can you help your athletes understand that they're capable of more than they realize?

104

Change or Die

Stephen Rassel

Minor League S&C Coordinator - Toronto Blue Jays

In his book Change or Die, Alan Deutschman references a popular study done by Dr. Edward Miller of Johns Hopkins.

Dr. Miller examined patients with heart disease severe enough to require bypass surgery, a procedure that temporarily relieves chest pain but often fails to prevent heart attacks or prolong lifespan. During his research, Dr. Miller had conversations with numerous patients in which he essentially told them, "If you don't change your lifestyle, you'll die."

Miller reports that although patients are told their chances of recovery hinge on lifestyle change, two years after surgeries, 90 percent of them have not implemented healthier routines. This statistic has been reinforced over and over again. To put it bluntly, they'd rather die than change their habits. Why?

Let's turn the spotlight on ourselves. How often have we planned to make changes in our lives only to fail at following through? Dr. Miller says we're not alone in regularly failing to execute on many of the goals we set for ourselves. Change is hard. Even in the most drastic "change or die" circumstances, even when the stakes could not climb any higher, adjusting one's established habits can seem almost impossible. But it's not.

Alan Deutschman advises three steps. First, build supportive relationships. Seek out accountability. Second, focus on developing new habits. Perform a task, repeat it, and reinforce it. Third, reframe your situation. This is a mental game. Keep the big picture in view. Remember you're not alone and that you have the strength necessary to achieve your goals.

Athlete Huddle

What's one habit that you've always meant to implement, but haven't yet?

Coach Huddle

How important is mental strength and dedication to athletic success? How can you be more intentional about training those skills in your athletes?

105

Hiking

Corliss Fingers

Director of Strength & Conditioning - Bethune Cookman University

This story was written by one of my former athletes:

I was in the High Sierra. It was a late snow year, so the drifts reached almost ten feet on top of some of the passes. Real mountaineering stuff.

I met up with a guy named Ajax and we decided we'd hike through the

rough parts together to stay safe. Ajax was just getting back from climbing Mt. Kilimanjaro, so I felt like he was a worthy partner. When he asked me about my myself, I said I was a goalkeeper for the Terps and a real badass. He told me he liked women's soccer and seemed to take my word for everything else. We climbed over Forester Pass at more than 13,000 feet. From the top, the view stretched out forever. We stood at the edge of a steep avalanche shoot, looking at the glacial tarn (partially frozen lake) before us, then down into the rest of the sweeping valley below. It was awesome but treacherous. We climbed down to a few hundred feet above the lake, and as we were about to begin our final traverse, we heard someone shouting, "Hey, how'd you get down there?"

We looked up and saw a guy in a t-shirt, with no ice axe, looking down at us with a bewildered expression. Once he reached our position, he explained that he was a novice and needed help reaching the end of the pass. We agreed.

Ten minutes later, we came to a boulder field. Ajax began making his way across. I waited for him to reach the other side and then began myself. About halfway across, I put my hand on a large boulder. As I did, I felt it shift and start to slide toward me. I thought, If this thing pins me and I have to cut off my arm like that kid in Utah, I'm gonna be pissed. So I was about to let it go and try to get away when I looked back and saw our rookie friend about 15 feet below me. He hadn't waited for me to clear the field. I knew that if I let go, there was a good chance the boulder would take him out. So I got underneath the boulder and held it with all my might. I shouted, "You've got ten seconds to get out of the way, and then I'm letting this go!" Now, at first I was really scared. But then I thought, I just spent three years getting my ass kicked by Corliss. This boulder's got nothing on her. Sure enough, I was able to hold it there until Muddy Noodle (that was his nickname by then) got to the other side of the boulder field. Then I let it go and ran like hell. It slid and crashed, taking part of the mountain with it into the icy lake.

So Corliss, thanks for the strength and the speed. Thanks for making it so that I didn't die and Muddy Noodle didn't have to get airlifted.

Athlete Huddle

When you leave this weight room, what do you take with you? What lessons learned here apply to the rest of life?

Coach Huddle

What will your athletes say about you in years to come? What do you hope they'll say?

106

How to Lose

Whitney Rodden

Head Strength & Conditioning Coach - MidAmerica Nazarene University

L osing can consume you if you let it. We've all experienced loss. We all know how it feels. Losing means you've identified a strategy that doesn't work. You know what not to do. After losing my little girl, I had many regrets, many memories of things I wished I'd done differently. But nobody can change what's already happened. All we can do is learn from our mistakes and implement corrections. Adversity will strike. That is certain. But when it does, will we allow the pain of loss to consume us, or will we learn the lesson and move on?

Strengthening your spirit can be even more important than strengthening your muscles. Being mentally prepared for any eventuality is critically important to your development as an athlete and a human being. We all know failure will come at some point. We'll experience loss, and when it comes, we won't be able to control it. But we can control our response. We can prep our bodies and minds to bounce back from the impact, to protect us from long-term harm. Staying in that space of loss keeps you from becoming the person God intends you to be. Your ability to cope with adversity can make all the difference between success and failure, not just for you, but for your teammates as well.

Athlete Huddle

Are you the friend or teammate who builds others up, or are you the one who stays in the funk and gloom of loss?

Coach Huddle

How do you respond to losing?

107

Reach

Angelo James

Owner - James Training Systems

I t's my first big meeting in my new position as the Director of Human Performance at Madison Academy, a small private school in Madison, Alabama. I know I need to dig deep and bring something memorable to grab the attention of the parents, students and coaches in attendance. Rather than going on a long rant about where I've been what I have done, I decide to challenge my audience with a simple, meaningful question.

"I want everyone in this room to raise their hands as high as they can!" Some people raise their hands just above their shoulders. Some raise their hands over their heads. Some fully extend their arms upward. "Okay," I continue. "Now I want you to reach just a little bit higher!" Naturally, most people who've not reached very high gain a few inches at this point.

"Alright, good! Now, can I ask everyone a simple question about what we just did? If you reached as high as you could the first time, how was it possible to raise your hand just a bit higher the second time? That is what I'm here to do. I am here to take what you already have and elevate it just a few inches! In the world of sport, a single inch is the difference between a blocked shot and a game-winning basket. It's the difference between the ball going in the goal and ricocheting off the post. It's the difference between a touchdown and a heartbreaking loss. Inches are everything. It's those who are willing to fight for that last inch in everything they do, day in and day out, who are successful. As your coach, my job is to take what you already have and challenge you to give a little bit more. "Now, let's try this again. Reach as high as you can!"

This time, the crowd gives a much better effort. But I know they've still got more. "Keep your hands up! What I have said holds true for the physical side of training. But what about the mental? If you raised your hand as high as you can, why are you still sitting down? That is another thing this program will do for you. It will change the way you think and how you approach challenges. How many of you even thought to stand up, or get on your tippy toes, or stand on your chair? I am here to challenge the way you approach your everyday life and to push, pull, shape, guide, squeeze, press, and challenge you to give your best, the first time we ask for it, every time we ask for it! Now, let's try this again. Reach!"

Athlete Huddle

Are you really giving your best, or do you only think you are?

Coach Huddle

What are some other ways you could demonstrate to your athletes the importance of maximum effort?

108

Choosing Greatness

Mike Caro

Head Strength & Conditioning Coach - Emory & Henry College

No one stumbles into greatness. No one rolls out of bed one morning, decides to win the Olympics or set a world record over breakfast, and simply does it. These goals are accomplished by people who choose to be great every day, the ones who stare daily obstacles in the face and push forward. As an athlete, you have to make the choice to be great every day, every drill, every set, every rep.

Being part of a team can be both a challenge and a benefit when it comes to greatness. The downside is that, like a chain with a weak link, if every member of the team isn't striving for greatness, the team can't be great. However, when a teammate is struggling, you can be their greatness. You can pick them up and help them push through. With a pat on the back and some positive encouragement, you can help them in their choice for greatness.

Becoming great requires you to continuously make a choice. It's an active choice, always needing to be reaffirmed. Do I want to commit myself to the sacrifice and hard work necessary to be better than mediocre? Those are the conditions for choosing greatness.

Choosing to be great is choosing to stand out. It doesn't guarantee fame or success or camaraderie. It's not about those things. It's about relentless improvement and getting the most from every opportunity you're given for the chance to achieve something rare. But it's not for everyone - only those who aren't satisfied with just being good. It's a choice that separates the "alright" from the elite. What will you choose?

Athlete Huddle

What are some of the ways you chose greatness recently? How will choosing greatness affect your athletic career?

Coach Huddle

Are you consistently choosing greatness? How are you providing your athletes and coworkers with opportunities to choose greatness?

109

Training vs. Trying

Dave Abernathy

Co-Founder/Director of Education & Sales - Tsunami Barbell/Total Strength & Speed

When competition season hits, athletes and coaches step onto various fields, courts and tracks, under stadium lights, seeking a prize for all the training that was put in during the offseason. For many athletes, training starts directly after each season ends. This body of work should include specific nutrition training plans, extensive strength training sessions, precise speed training sessions, position skill training, and film training.

Notice that the common denominator is training - not to be mistaken with trying. Training, as it relates to our field, is a lifestyle of discipline that establishes confidence for athletes and coaches to go out and compete. Trying literally means to make an attempt at something, to put something to the test or trial. We can try all we want, but if we are unprepared, succeeding relies on one's natural ability. Natural ability may take some further than others, but why would we limit ourselves to only access the gifts we were born with?

I was reading recently about the city of Corinth, home to the Greek Isthmus Games. In 1 Corinthians, Paul, formerly known as Saul of Tarsus, references these games. "Everyone who competes in the games goes into strict training...I strike a blow to my body and make it my slave so that after

I have preached to others, I myself will not be disqualified for the prize," (1 Cor. 9:26-27, NIV). To run in the Greek games, a runner was required to train for ten months. If they had not done so, they were disqualified from competing. The point wasn't just to see who could win the prize, but to see who had the discipline to endure those ten months. Paul is speaking of the daily consistency it takes to live a disciplined lifestyle. He knew living a life of faith was about living it daily, not just leaving it up to trying when tested. And it's the same with competing in these games today. It's about the life you lead every day, the training you put in when you're not under the lights.

Before cell phones with high-tech cameras, we had old wind-up film cameras. You would have to take your film to the drugstore to get developed in a darkroom. If the film was exposed to light too soon, your pictures were ruined. In these days of instant gratification, selfies and everyone wanting to be in their own version of the limelight, we have to remember the importance of both process and darkness. Because most times training goes unseen. Before social media, it was never seen. People who come to football games don't care about what happened before the lights came on. All that matters to them is what happens on the field.

There are numerous 5:30 am training sessions that will go unseen, your will tested to its limits time and again, possibly with no one around to notice. But at the right time, if we don't give up, what was done in the dark will come to light. Embrace the dark so that when the lights do come on, your picture turns out. Keep training.

Athlete Huddle

When was a time you failed to do the work in the dark and it came out under the lights?

Coach Huddle

What are some ways you could promote discipline and patience in your athletes?

110

Three Feet From Gold

Lorenzo Guess

Associate Head S&C Coach/Director of Player Enrichment - Michigan State University

I got this story from the Better Life Coaching Blog. To me, it says a lot about the power of perseverance. Nobody knows the future, and in the end, success belongs to those who stay the course. So keep digging!

"In his all-time classic book, Think and Grow Rich, Napoleon Hill tells the story of R. U. Harby.

"Harby's uncle had gold fever, so he staked his claim and started digging. After a lot of hard work, he found a vein of ore, so he covered it up and returned home to raise money for the machinery he would need to work the mine.

"Darby and his uncle raised the money and returned to the site to make their fortune. Things started well and before long, they had enough to clear their debts. Everything else was profit. Things were looking good!

"Then the supply of gold stopped. The vein of ore disappeared. They kept on digging, but they found nothing. After a while, they quit in frustration and sold their machinery to a junk man for a few hundred dollars. The astute junk man called in a mining engineer, who checked the mine and calculated that there was a vein of gold just three feet from where

Darby and his uncle had stopped digging. The junk man went on to make millions.

"Darby returned home, paid back everyone who had lent him money and determined to learn from his mistake. He went on to become a phenomenally successful insurance salesman, more than recouping what he would have made from the gold mine. He learned the lesson that you need to persevere through difficulties and stay focused if you are to become successful. Whenever you feel like giving up on your dream, remember that you may be just three feet from gold!"

Athlete Huddle

Do you have a growth mindset? How easily do you succumb to frustration? Can you think of a time when your hard work paid bigger dividends than you expected?

Coach Huddle

When was the last time you emphasized to your athletes the need for perseverance? How do you train mental toughness?

111

Burn Your Ships

Jeremy Boone

Owner - WinningLeader.io

In the year 1519, Captain Hernan Cortes arrived in Veracruz, the New World, with six hundred men. Upon arrival, he gave the order to his men to burn the ships. The message was sent loud and clear. There was no turning back.

Cortes put himself and his men in a position to either succeed or to die. Quitting was not an option. Retreating was not an option. The result? Two years later, he succeeded in his conquest of the Aztec empire.

There will be times when you and I will be called to abandon our own ships. And unless you burn your ships, and don't opt to play it safe, you may never truly know what you are capable of. If you leave your ships in the harbor, it sends a message that you aren't fully committed. Instead, be willing to overcome your fear and use it as fuel to march forward with greatness.

Athlete Huddle

What ships do you need to burn in your pursuit of consistently performing your best? Your ships can come in the form of a habit, an attitude, a belief, etc. Yes, it will feel scary, but that's when you will feel most alive. The bigger the risk, the bigger the reward. Your team needs you to burn your ships.

Coach Huddle

What ships do you need to burn in your program? Are you stuck doing the same thing the same way year after year? Do you have an impression or belief about a staff member or athlete that is preventing you from developing that relationship? As a coach, I love this story because it's a fantastic example of the relationship between environmental design and your athlete's mindset. Sometimes, we need to change the environment, or a variable of the environment, in order to get the most out of the athletes we work with every day. How can you redesign your current environment to get even more out of your athletes?

112

The Power of a Penny

Matt Nein

Coordinator of Sports Performance - Salisbury University

L et's say you're walking down the street and you see a penny. Do you pick it up? Probably not, right? Most people wouldn't. What about a dollar bill? Most people would. What's the difference? It's a question of value. A dollar is worth more. But which is more common? Pennies are.

So here's what we know. One hundred pennies make up one dollar, and we tend to see way more pennies on the ground than dollars. Obviously, you can't buy much with a single penny, but they add up. So you can start picking up pennies with the guarantee that you'll have a dollar once you gather one hundred of them, or you can wait and hope for the rare dollar bill.

In life, we rarely focus on the little things that can guarantee our success. We see minimal return on our investment, so we tend to ignore the opportunities. We walk by the penny without picking it up. We focus on the goals we're pursuing, and yet we refuse to take advantage of the small habits than inch us forward. We want the outcome but not the process.

Let the penny be a symbol of our willingness to embrace the little things, the minute tasks that promise success as they add up over time. Let your willingness to walk by a penny remind you not to ignore the details. Details matter. My challenge to you is to never pass up a penny again. Identify the little things that can push you forward to achieving your potential. And do them. Do them with vigor, excitement, and passion. Embrace the process, not as a frustrating, monotonous series of meaningless tasks, but as your opportunity to build a reputation. Build your character. Build your journey one penny at a time. You'll be amazed at how much it adds up. More importantly, you'll be very content with the path you'll have taken.

Athlete Huddle

Describe how you feel when you've invested time in something nobody wanted to do.

Coach Huddle

Identify five areas where you can invest in the details and make yourself better.

113

Chop

Marisa Viola

Assistant Director of Performance & Education - PLAE

A man wakes up in the middle of a thick forest. He feels an axe in his hand, but the sky is dark. He can't see anything. There's no food, no water, no light. What does he do? He's desperate to escape the forest, but he calms himself, evaluates his situation, and reaches out until he feels the trunk of a tree in front of him. Then he swings his axe. Chop! He reaches out again and feels where his axe fell. He swings again. Chop! Coolly, patiently, he feels the tree. Then what? He takes a few steps in the dark and touches another tree. Chop! He continues his work, one step at a time, one swing at a time, one tree at a time, until he reaches the edge of the forest.

In sport, we have repetitive actions. Tackles, kicks, passes, shots, etc. Athletes practice these moves over and over again, because when the time comes to execute in competition, they know distractions will be present. Distractions are always present. But if an athlete can address one intention at a time, if he or she can maintain laser focus on the task at hand, chances are that success will come.

What if the man in the forest has food? Does he take a break to eat? What if he has light? Does he look for a shortcut through the trees? Probably. We tend to rely on the precautions we take. But as the woodcutter teaches us, the most direct route to success requires that we focus solely and completely on the job that lies before us. Eliminate distractions and excuses. Whether in the weight room, in practice, or in competition, let your mind be consumed by the tree in front of you, by the swing you're taking. Focus on one chop at a time and watch your forest fall.

Athlete Huddle

What are the distractions you need to eliminate in the weight room, in practice, in games, etc.? How are you going to get rid of them?

Coach Huddle

How can you help your athletes to focus on one chop at a time if you're preoccupied with other matters? How will you set an example of being present and laser focused for those who look up to you?

114

4-Minute Mile

Noel Durfey

Head Football Sports Performance Coach - Duke University

I've always found Roger Bannister's 4-minute mile a great event to point to when telling student-athletes not to talk themselves out of what they're able to achieve. For years, experts had been saying the 4-minute mile was impossible for the human body to achieve, even dangerous. In 1940, the record was pushed to 4:01. That stood for 9 years. People thought the human body had reached its limit.

On May 6, 1954, Roger Bannister ran the mile in 3:59:4. Less than 1 year later, someone else ran a sub-4-minute mile. Thirteen months later, three more runners in one race ran a mile in under four minutes. Between 1954 and 1960, 24 runners did what was once thought impossible, even dangerous.

Once Bannister broke the barrier, others then began to believe that it was possible. Humans are amazing, adaptive organisms. If we are not self-limiting, we are able to accomplish many tasks that may be thought impossible. To make ourselves grow, both physically and mentally, we must continually stretch or wipe out our perceived limits.

Athlete Huddle

Identify one thing that you think is impossible for you to accomplish, but that you've dreamed of accomplishing. How are you going to wipe out your perceived limits and make it happen?

Coach Huddle

Do you encourage your athletes to reach for the stars? Or are you holding them back, telling them that their dreams are impossible?

115

Seedtime and Harvest

Marty Barnett

Director of Strength & Conditioning - Rejoice Christian School (OK)

G od is the same today, yesterday, and forever. "As long as the Earth endures, seedtime and harvest, cold and heat, summer and winter, day and night will never cease," (NIV, Gen. 8.22). We can count on that. His promises are constant. We can count on that too. One of these promises is "seedtime and harvest." So just as God promises Noah in Genesis, He also promises us that if we sow at the right time a harvest will come. The truth is a double edge sword. The good news is we can reap a harvest. The bad news is that sowing seeds isn't always easy and the harvest can sometimes be a long way off.

Soren Kierkegaard said, "Patience is necessary, and one cannot reap immediately where one has sown." Patience can be a difficult virtue for most. Sowing seeds and putting in the work, oftentimes, isn't the difficult part. It's the waiting. In that same vein, Robert Louis Stevenson writes, "Don't judge each day by the harvest you reap but by the seeds that you plant."

We should judge our days by the process of sowing and not focus on the harvest. Harvest time will come. We can count on it if we sow. However, we must be careful what we are sowing, as the quality and type of seed are crucial to success during the harvest. Galatians 6 cautions, "Do not be deceived. God cannot be mocked. A man reaps what he sows. Whoever sows to please their flesh, from the flesh will reap destruction; whoever sows to please the Spirit, from the Spirit will reap eternal life."

Athlete Huddle

Are your efforts and attitudes going to reap the harvest you want? How can you speak into your teammates to help them sow the effort and attitudes you need to be successful as a team?

Coach Huddle

How can we speak into our athletes about sowing and reaping in their lives? Are we setting a good example for our team in these areas? Where can we do better?

116

Rob Brokaw

Money in the Bank

Strength Coach - North Bend Central High School (NE)

uilding strength is a lot like building up your finances. Being from Omaha, I like to point to Warren Buffet. Warren is famous for being one of the richest men who's ever lived. He's been quoted numerous times, but a few stick out in my mind in relation to strength.

1. "Always invest for the long term."

We need to think long term about training. There is no camp, no workout, no program that will make you strong. Look at it this way. Let's put a $5 value on our daily investment of training, nutrition and sleep. For everything you've done up to this point, I'll spot you $1,000. With an interest rate of 1 percent that will compound daily, when you focus, that $5 daily investment will turn into $2,700 after the first year, $4,400 after the second, $6,150 after the third, $7,900 after the fourth, $9,700 after fifth, and $11,500 after the sixth.

That brings us to our next quote.

2. "No matter how great your talent or efforts, some things just take time."

Strength is a skill. You have to work at it. Develop it. You can be super talented or incredibly gritty and hard-working, but that still doesn't mean strength will happen overnight for you. Strength takes time to build but the good news is, to quote Coach Ausmus, "It won't come off in the shower."

3. "Time is the friend of the wonderful, the enemy of the mediocre."

Buffet sees the amount of money in the bank as a way to keep score. Who has been putting in the daily work and who hasn't? I think that applies directly to what we are doing here in the weight room. For the people that do the work, it shows in competition. And those who haven't get surpassed by those that do.

Athlete Huddle

What are your investments looking like? Are you thinking long term?

Coach Huddle

The process promises success over time. What is stopping you from acting on it?

117

The First Time You Quit

Jerry Palmieri

34 Year Veteran NFL/NCAA S&C Coach - Super Bowl Champion XLII and XLVI

One of the most disrespected individuals in athletics is the quitter. When I say quitter, I'm not referring to the athlete who finishes the season and then decides to leave the game so he can pursue other passions. Nor am I referring to the coach who chooses to step away so he or she can spend more time with family. A quitter is someone who fails to fulfill an obligation. It's the athlete that leaves the team in the midst of a difficult season. It's the athlete who drops out of the conditioning session or pulls up before the finish line. It's the lifter who tells his coach he did all three sets when he only completed two. It's the coach who stops grinding to prepare his team when he realizes they won't make the playoffs. No one respects a quitter.

Remember this thought. The first time you quit will be the hardest. The first time you miss practice is the hardest. The first time you don't finish a set is the hardest. The first is always the hardest. After that, it gets easier and easier. This principle holds true in life, as well. The first time you walk away from your spouse is the hardest. The first time you lie, steal, abuse a family member, cheat on your taxes, or deceive your business partner will be the hardest.

That's why it is so important to hold fast. Cling to your convictions. Stand tall for what you believe in. Don't lower your standards because you are facing difficult circumstances. Persevere through adversity. Remember, the first time you quit will be the hardest.

Athlete Huddle

What are the convictions that you build your life on? How can you show respect for those convictions in your approach to training?

Coach Huddle

What kind of example are you setting for your athletes, not just in the weight room, but in life as well?

118

The Final Blow

Tim Anderson

Co Founder - Original Strength Systems

A man wanted to move a boulder on his property, but he wasn't strong enough to move it himself and he didn't have any strong farm animals or heavy machinery. What he did have was a sledgehammer and a determination to move that rock. He believed if he could break the rock into smaller pieces, he would be able to move it away. So, the man set out every day to swing his sledgehammer at the boulder.

Every day, he would spend 30 minutes in the morning hitting the rock, working his hammer from side to side like a sword. And every day, the rock remained the same. Nothing happened. But the man did not give up. Days came and went. Weeks turned into months. But the man's resolve did not change. In his mind, he knew he could bust the rock into smaller pieces and then move it.

Then, one morning, in the third month, the man noticed a crack forming in the middle of the boulder. The man became excited and began to hit the rock with a ferocious intensity. And then it happened. The boulder split in two. The man was filled with joy and he released a yell of victory. But his joy was soon followed with a weird sense of sadness. His old friend, the rock, had been defeated. The dance they enjoyed every morning was over. The man dropped his head and looked down at his hammer, which he was still holding in his hands. His gaze shifted to his hands and his forearms. They had become rippled with muscle. They looked as if they were carved out of the very stone he had been battling every day, as did his shoulders and his torso. Like the boulder, he too had changed. After his musing, the man reached down, hugged one of the newly formed rocks, hoisted it onto his shoulder and walked away with it. He then came and retrieved the other half.

A friend later asked him, "How were you able to hit that rock every day? Why didn't you just give up and find another way to move it?" The man replied, "I could see it breaking in my head. Even before the first blow, I knew I could break that rock. I could see it in my mind every day."

His friend then said, "It took you three months! Do you know how many hits it took to bust the boulder?"

The man replied, "Yes. It took all of them."

Athlete Huddle

What if success was just one more attempt, rep, or effort away? What if the only thing keeping you from being successful was your resolve and determination to keep moving forward?

Coach Huddle

Do you have a vision that you are able to hold onto when you feel like you are not making any progress?

119

Team Unity

Bryan Miller

Associate S&C Coach and Sports Science Coordinator - United States Naval Academy

D eveloping a sense of togetherness in a group of 110 individuals can be quite a challenge, especially when those individuals have egos, especially when they're each incredibly unique. I've found it takes an open mind and willingness to cooperate. Most importantly, it takes trust.

Let's make this visual. Take a couple of footballs and throw them to players in the weight room. Have those players pass around the balls until every member of the team has touched one. How do you measure that? It's tricky. How long does it take? It probably takes a while. Let's consider an alternative approach. Put your two team captains in the center of the room and hand them the two footballs. Now split the team into halves and arrange each group around one of the captains, right arms extended, reaching into the huddles, slowly drawing closer and closer. Now have those captains turn, touching each player's hand with their footballs.

Which approach was more efficient? The second one, right? Team unity can only be built if we place the burden of leadership, literally and figuratively, in the hands of our team leaders. If we all come together, shoulder to shoulder, extending our helping hands for the good of the team, we'll achieve more as a unit than any of us ever could have as individuals.

Athlete Huddle

Captains, do you really understand the impact that you have on your team?

Coach Huddle

What exercises are you using with your athletes to demonstrate the importance of togetherness?

120

"I Noticed…"

Jeff Friday

Assistant Strength & Conditioning Coach - Cincinnati Bengals

We all have dealt with an athlete or coworker who was "difficult." Somebody who wanted to do something their way, on their terms. That usually results in conflict, doesn't it?

I had one such player. To reduce conflict, I realized that I had to develop a better relationship with him. One strategy I tried was to commend him for positive things I noticed in his personal life. I'd begin with "I noticed…" According to research, such practice improves cooperation because of the personal connection it creates. If the athlete exhibited a good work ethic in the weight room, I would acknowledge that quality and

say, "I noticed you worked hard in the weight room today." If he elevated

the group by his performance or encouragement, I would say, "I noticed

you encouraged others and made them better."

Life is filled with moments. This strategy heightened my awareness of commendable behaviors, as well as opportunities to praise them. How many chances do we miss to build bridges because we're not in the moment? Or do we sometimes notice good traits but fail to acknowledge them?

After a few weeks of this intervention, I noticed a change in the relationship. There appeared to be less conflict. That could just be my perception, but the important point is that I decided to work on myself and take responsibility for my part in the relationship.

Athlete Huddle

Do you celebrate your teammates' successes even if they overshadow yours? Do you regularly encourage and praise those around you?

Coach Huddle

How could you be more active in your verbal appreciation of your athletes? How could you be more specific in your encouragement of their personal behaviors?

121

You Are What You Eat

Eric Overland

Supervisor of Strength & Conditioning - Wayne State University

Sometimes it's easy to eliminate bad influences. We just remove them or we walk away. Other times it's not that simple. We feel unable to separate ourselves from an environment, even though we're aware it's unhealthy for us. What do we do when a situation seems devoid of any apparent solution?

We've all heard the saying, "You are what you eat." I'm a firm believer in this. But for now, let's paint a different picture. Let's imagine a bowl of water. It has to stay filled to the brim. The problem is that the water is dirty. How do you clean it? You can't dump it out. You can't scoop it out. You have to pour an abundance of clean water into it. The more clean water you add, the more dirty water will spill over. It may take a while, but eventually, the clean will have completely replaced the dirty.

So it is in life. Dirt can't simply be removed; it must be replaced. Whether it's a bad relationship, a negative environment, a challenging circumstance, or anything else, the more positives you pour into your life, the more you'll see the dirt spill away. Seek out real, honest, life-giving experiences. Pour your energies and focus into them. Identify relationships that keep you encouraged, humble, accountable and joyful. Watch yourself grow.

Athlete Huddle

Identify the dirty water in your bowl. What will you replace it with?

Coach Huddle

What can we do to ensure we're pouring clean water into our athletes' lives?

122

Coach 'Em All

Craig Fitzgerald

Director of Strength & Conditioning
for Football - University of Tennessee

att "Mad Dog" McDonald was a football player at Catholic University in the late 1990s. I was fortunate to coach him as Catholic's special teams coach and strength coach. At the Division 3 level, strength and conditioning was optional for players. Most of them would train hard during the academic year and then take the summer off. This one particular summer, we had a handful of underused, underappreciated athletes stay and train with us on campus. Their leader was Mad Dog.

Our summer training group met every Monday, Tuesday, Thursday and

Friday for two months. The training would start at 6 pm and wrap up close to 9 pm. We would start on the track and run for an hour, then hit our tiny, no-ventilation, coffin-like weight room for almost two hours. After a long day at their construction jobs or internships, the guys would feed on the group's camaraderie, as well as the games they would create. Whether it was a final sprint on the track, a high box jump race or a top set power clean, the group would make a competition out of it. Mad Dog was the lightning rod behind it all, seeking to fire up his teammates and push them past their limits. Mad Dog himself was an undersized reserve linebacker and backup special teams role player at Catholic before summer training began. By the end of the summer, he'd gained 15 lbs. of body weight, increased his squat by 100 lbs. and improved his box jump by 6 inches.

Matt's physical improvements are amazing. But what's more amazing is the way the whole group improved alongside him.

We had one guy increase his power clean by 50 lbs. We had two receivers drop their 40-yard dash times by three tenths. It was my first year as a strength coach, so all I knew were the basics of clean, squat, bench, jump and sprint. I say that to demonstrate just how key a role Matt's leadership played that summer.

We tested the whole team in all the lifts and conditioning when the school year started. Every coach commented on how great the local group looked. Each of those guys met with a lot of success in training camp and played a significant role throughout the season. Matt became our special teams captain, leading us to a 10-0 regular season and the Division 3 playoffs.

As I write this today, the members of that small summer group have gone

on to be successful professionals, great husbands and great fathers. Matt married his college sweetheart and became a United States Marine, serving in active duty for twenty years. He is a high ranking leader in the Corps who focuses on helping his fellow Marines, not gaining rank. His close friends have told me that Matt has turned down many promotions in order to stay active in the field with his men.

When I think about Matt, I am humbled that I had the chance to be a part of his football story. Some strength coaches are searching for the next great NFL prospect. But I continue to hit that weight room each day, keeping my heart open and looking for the next Matt "Mad Dog" McDonald.

Athlete Huddle

What does it mean to lead? How could you be a better teammate to those around you, one who'd be remembered for years to come?

Coach Huddle

What does it mean to lead by example? How can you demonstrate your commitment to your athletes? How can you earn their trust?

123

Trust Bank

Mitch Hauschildt

Prevention, Rehab & Physical Performance Coordinator - Missouri State University

We all know what banks do. They store and keep your money safe and sound. When used properly, banks can help you grow your money and life savings into large sums. Wealth is built when you invest in your bank accounts with consistent, intentional deposits that earn interest over time.

We also have bank accounts in our relationships. These accounts exist to help us understand how we should trust, interact and work with those around us. In order to have solid, substantial, and trustworthy

relationships, we have to make consistent and intentional deposits into them. Deposits into our relationship bank accounts come in the form of actions and statements that build trust. When we make these consistent and intentional deposits over long periods of time, we build strong relationships that lead to success in all aspects of life.

Deposits come in the form of words of affirmation, kind acts, sacrifices, hard work, focused efforts, and anything that shows love and respect to those around us. Negative words, laziness, dishonesty, selfishness, and unkind acts are all examples of withdrawals from that relational bank account.

Withdrawals are counterproductive to the goal of developing trust with those around us. Trust is fundamental to all high-quality relationships. Trust is important to a team. Teammates need to know that each person is willing to put in the work and do the things that need to be done in order to succeed when times get tough.

When teammates make consistent and intentional deposits into their team's trust bank accounts, their likelihood of success rises exponentially. Teams that work and play for each other are almost always successful. Making deposits early and often with your teammates, coaches, instructors and family is a winning strategy.

Athlete Huddle

How could you invest today in your relationships with your teammates?

Coach Huddle

Are you making deposits or withdrawals from your organization's trust bank? How could you encourage your athletes to make regular, intentional deposits into their relationships with each other?

124

Strength To Serve

David Jack

Owner - Activprayer

Stories of weight room heroics, metrics and personal records leave the gym constantly. But ten years down the road, few people care about them, especially if they're full of bragging. People smell that stuff a mile away, and they tend to avoid it.

Instead of just your stories leaving the weight room, what if your strength did? It does you and those around you no good when it's stuck in some bar, rack, bell or sled in the training room. Getting physically stronger requires focus, discipline and diligence, and those are the values that should be shared. How much someone lifts matters way less than why he or she lifts it. Those values last a lifetime. If you're training for the applause, the high fives and the pride you feel when you tell the stories, that strength fades quickly.

If you really want your strength to last, consider the people in your family, your community, and on your team who need you to serve with your strength. Carry something that's too heavy for someone else. Stand in the gap for those who can't. Speak up when no one else will. Hold back words that make others weak. That's real strength. Honor it in the gym. It's a sacred gift. Pursue it and take the lessons that your journey teaches into the world with you. Give them away, not for applause or respect, but because others need them.

Strength isn't strong at all when you have to call attention to it. Make it about others. Those are the stories worth telling. Those are the stories people want to hear. Those are the things that last.

So decide what kind of strength you're aiming for. Chase it as hard as you can. Earn it and then give it away.

Athlete Huddle

What kind of strong do you want to be?

Coach Huddle

What kind of strength are you coaching?

125

Weed and Feed

Zach Mathers

Director of Strength & Conditioning/Head Athletic Trainer - University of Sioux Falls

We as coaches and athletes know that the mental game is just as important as the physical one. We spend a lot of time strengthening our bodies, hardening our muscles and honing motor skills. We may even have a process that mentally prepares us for competition. But what about when the game is over? What about when the season is over. We place a lot of emphasis on keeping the body sharp during those interims, but what about the mind?

I like to think of the human mind as a garden. Good thoughts are planted. Bad thoughts are weeds; they spring up spontaneously, unsummoned and hard to kill. Eventually, if you don't weed your garden, those bad thoughts will take over and spoil the land. And if you do, you still have to water and fertilize your good thoughts. Plant enough of them and the weeds will have nowhere to grow. This is a simple principle, but it's truth is profound. Mental strength and positivity can be trained, just like you practice running, blocking and catching. It's a process that always works. Positivity is a choice. Make sure you're choosing correctly each day. Build that habit.

Athlete Huddle

Give an example of a challenge you encountered during today's workout and how you worked through it? What are two good things you saw from your teammates today?

Coach Huddle

What are three great things you noticed about today's session?

126

Whose Job Is It?

Matt Jennings

Head Strength & Conditioning Coach - Xavier University

I'm not sure who authored this little anecdote, but it's stuck with me since I first encountered it. It's about four people: Everybody, Somebody, Anybody, and Nobody.

There was an important job to be done. Everybody was sure that Somebody would do it. Anybody could, but Nobody did. Everybody was responsible, but the job remained undone. So Somebody got mad. Everybody thought Anybody could step in. Nobody expected Everybody to remain uninvolved. In the end, Everybody blamed Somebody. Nobody did anything. Anybody could. And the job never got done.

Does this sound familiar? Humans are experts at displacing blame. We're great at criticizing the actions of others. But we rarely take the initiative to step out in front of everyone else to address an issue that needs addressing. The individual who does so is uncommonly valuable.

Athlete Huddle

What does being a leader mean? Who are the leaders in your life, on your team, etc.? When does a situation require you to assume a leadership role?

Coach Huddle

How can you create opportunities for each of your athletes to develop leadership skills?

127

Walking the Tightrope

Grant Geib

Director of Football Strength & Conditioning - Western Michigan University

At the forefront of athletic contests are displays of extraordinary physical ability. But those in the trenches know that it's often the mental component of sport that separates the good from the great. Confidence is paramount in elite athletes. They possess an unshakable faith in themselves that constantly pushes their physical thresholds. This translates into unbelievable performances that inspire and excite audiences. We have all seen moments in sport so charged and exhilarating that they walked the line between possible and impossible. Those moments occur when the athletes and coaches behind them choose to believe.

Charles Blondin was the most famous tightrope walker of his time. He completed impossible feats for a living. At one point in his career, he pushed a wheelbarrow containing 350 pounds of cement along a tightrope suspended over Niagara Falls. Accounts of the event say he purposely completed the task slowly and often faked losing his balance to keep the audience engaged. However, Blondin was in complete control and never doubted for a second that he would make it to the other side.

After successfully tightrope walking the falls (he was the first to ever do it), Blondin was bombarded with cheers from media and fans.

When the questions died down, he asked a question of the audience. "Who here believes that I can do it again?"

A man stepped forward and claimed, "I think you can do it again!"

Blondin demanded, "Do you think I can do it again or do you believe that I can do it again."

The man replied, "What's the difference?"

Blondin walked over to his wheelbarrow and tipped it over, sending cement bricks crashing onto the ground. He then pushed the empty contraption over to the man and said, "If you think I can do it, you

can stand here and watch. But if you believe I can do it, jump in the wheelbarrow."

There are two points here. The first is that the tightrope walker had full confidence in his own ability. He believed that he would accomplish his goal, even when nobody else did. He made the impossible possible. The second point is that you can only "jump in" if you believe. If you are going to be "all in" as a team, everybody needs to be fully invested in the mission. Everybody must climb into the wheelbarrow. As we train our bodies to pursue our goals, we must train our minds to believe that we'll achieve them. This is the only way to walk the tightrope that leads to victory.

Athlete Huddle

Have a teammate's actions ever inspired you to "jump in?" Do you believe you have the power to achieve your goals?

Coach Huddle

Do your athletes believe in themselves? If not, how can you stimulate mental growth to get them there?

128

Speak Softly and Carry a Big Stick

Fred Hale

Co-Director of Sports Performance - Eastern Michigan University

President Theodore Roosevelt once said, "Speak softly and carry a big stick. You will go far." He was referring to his foreign policy, which was nicknamed "Big Stick Diplomacy." Roosevelt believed in the value of meekness. He tended toward forbearance and non aggression when dealing with other nations, but backed up his peaceful words with an indisputable show of strength.

How often have you heard other teams or opponents brag? Do they ever get obnoxious? Would you say they speak softly? Probably not, right? In many cases, an abundance of confidence accompanies abundance of ego, and that sometimes causes athletes or teams to paint targets on their backs. Wouldn't it be better to let your performance speak for itself? Those who speak softly fly under the radar until it's time to compete. Those who refrain from bragging (even when they have a reason to brag) garner a lot more respect than those who talk big and can't back up their words.

You see this all the time. The favored team gets beat by the scrappy underdog. The challenger knocks down the champion heavyweight. Confidence is a good thing. But sport is littered with examples of pride paving the way for humiliation. My advice is the same as Roosevelt's. Let your game speak for you. Speak softly. Carry a big stick. Know your abilities. Be confident. Stare down any challenge without fear. You'll go far.

Athlete Huddle

Do you spend more time talking about how good you are or working to improve? Who comes to mind when you think of quiet strength? Do you respect that quality?

Coach Huddle

Does your example encourage humility or arrogance? How are you teaching your athletes to respond to intimidation?

129

Finding Focus

Nick Winkelman

Head of Athletic Performance & Science - Irish Rugby Football Union

Coaches, here's an exercise you can use in your weight rooms to show your athletes the value of mental focus. Gather them together before a session and pose the following question.

As we consider the challenge before us, how can we ensure we use this time to optimally improve our performance?

Your athletes' answers may vary, but one thing is certain: If they're not focused on the work they put in, then they should expect underdeveloped skills and inconsistent results.

Ask for a volunteer. When he steps forward, have him extend his stronger arm out in front of him. Tell him to imagine he's made of steel. So when you press down on his wrist, his arm shouldn't move.

Then press down, gently at first, but gradually increasing in force until some movement is visible. You'll probably find it difficult to move his arm through any significant range of motion.

Ask your athlete how he felt. He'll most likely respond that he felt pretty strong, which may elicit a few snickers from his teammates. But the point is, he was strong. Express to the group that because he placed all of his focus on remaining motionless, he succeeded to the best of his ability.

Now address your volunteer again. This time, in addition to keeping his extended arm still, he must count backward from 100, out loud, by twos. Also, he's to follow your moving index finger with his eyes. Go!

This time, as you press down on his wrist, he'll feel immediately weaker. As your finger moves and his eyes follow, he'll struggle to count. Encourage him to keep going! As his focus wanes, his arm lowers under the pressure you're applying.

Now ask him how he felt the second time. He'll probably say much weaker, right? Explain to your athletes that just as you effectively reduced your volunteer's strength by introducing distraction, so any training session can be compromised by lack of focus.

Always remember that your mind manages your strength. Encourage your athletes to individually identify what winning looks like in any given training session. Encourage them to focus on that alone. Any other decision places them and their team at a disadvantage.

Athlete Huddle

What strategies could you employ to ensure you maintain your focus on the task at hand while training?

Coach Huddle

What strategies could you employ to continually promote the importance of focus in your weight room?

130

The Chinese Bamboo Tree

Ron McKeefery

Vice President of Performance & Education - PLAE

Sport is often like the story of the Chinese bamboo tree. It starts with a little seed, which you plant, water and fertilize. For a whole year, you tend the earth where that seed is planted. And for a whole year, nothing happens. So you continue on. You water and fertilize that earth. Still nothing. Not so much as a sprout.

Year three is the same. And even year four. Does this sound familiar? How many times have you struggled against the sneaking suspicion that your hard work is futile? How many seemingly lost causes have you almost given up on? At what point do you cut your losses and begin applying your efforts in other directions? We've all been there.

But in the fifth year after the Chinese bamboo tree is planted, something happens. Something very noticeable. The tree sprouts and springs into the sky. In six short weeks, it grows ninety feet.

The point is that hard work is rarely futile. Lack of gains can feel discouraging, even debilitating, especially over a long period of time. You see people cutting corners, getting away with things. Your testing numbers are disappointing. Maybe you're not getting as many minutes of game time as you were hoping for. At a certain point, you have to make a decision whether you're going to continue on or quit. That is your big moment. That is where you separate yourself from everyone else by making an unlikely choice and sticking with something that hasn't seemed to pay off. That's where you build character and develop grit. Persistence is the story of the Chinese bamboo. People eventually reap what they sow, and those who plant diligence will reap success.

Athlete Huddle

Do you relate to this story? Are you actually watering your bamboo or just waiting for it to grow?

Coach Huddle

How many times have you felt that you weren't getting through to an athlete? Give an example of a time you were about to give up, but didn't.

131

Thermostat vs. Thermometer

Adam Feit

Coordinator of Physical and Mental Performance - Springfield College

As coaches, we do everything we can to control the outcome. A personal record, a win on the scoreboard, a spot on the roster. We work hard, coach harder and try to somehow manipulate every little variable to ensure success.

But the truth is, things that are meant to happen will happen, and we have to demonstrate and teach the resiliency to keep on keeping on, regardless of how the cards are played.

When adversity strikes, we can make one of two choices:

1. We can respond by keeping the standard and staying true to our beliefs and actions. We can maintain our course and not let the opinions and actions of sheep affect our wolf mentality.

2. We can react and let other opinions and actions affect who we are and how we play. We can play down to their level, feel sorry for ourselves and move our mindset from warrior to wounded.

When that curveball gets thrown, we can strike out or slam it out. I opt for the latter. I want you to look at a thermometer when it becomes hot outside. What does it do? It goes up, right? What about when it's cold outside? It goes down. A thermometer reacts to its environment. As the environment changes, so does the thermometer.

But what does a thermostat do? Whether it's hot or cold, the thermostat never changes. It doesn't respond to outside conditions. It doesn't give in to the environment around it. Rather, a thermostat sets the temperature. It sets the standard. It sets the tone.

Remember. The next time something outside your control comes into your life and tries to take over, what will you do? Will you be a thermostat or a thermometer?

Athlete Huddle

Do you react to adversity or impose your will? Do you set the temperature for your teammates? Do you set the temperature for your season?

Coach Huddle

What situations at home and work trigger you to behave more like a thermometer than a thermostat?

132

Conductors vs. Resistors

Zach Mather

Director of Strength & Conditioning/Head Athletic Trainer - University of Sioux Falls

Electricians know that conductors move energy and resistors don't. Resistors hold onto power and conductors let go. How does this apply to people? Well, some individuals resent when others succeed. They hold back their praise. They refuse to celebrate. They absorb energy and hold onto it. They're stingy. Others, on the other hand, possess enough humility to let energy pass through them. They let go, and in so doing, they deliver massive amounts of power to those around them. They may not generate it themselves. But because they're willing to be conduits, they become key ingredients of successful teams.

A resistor relies on his own power. His pride keeps him from accessing other sources. But a conductor empties himself of ego so he can participate in something greater. Which one are you?

Athlete Huddle

When was the last time you saw a teammate exhibit the qualities of a conductor?

Coach Huddle

How can we be better conductors for our fellow coaches?

133

The Farmer

Scott Sinclair

Director of Football Strength & Conditioning - University of Georgia

A farmer had an old mule that fell into a deep well. Looking down at the trapped animal, he mopped his forehead and considered how hard he'd have to work to rescue it. The mule looked back up at him. He's tired, the farmer thought. He's lived a good life. He doesn't have much longer. So the farmer fetched his shovel, planning to bury the mule alive.

He tossed a scoop of dirt into the well, then another. Then another. An hour passed. The farmer ventured to the edge of the hole and looked down, expecting to see the mule nearly covered. But the resourceful animal had been shaking the incoming soil off its back and packing it down, raising itself up inch by inch. Surprised, the farmer returned to his work, and before long, the mule stepped safely out of the well.

Here's the point. You can defeat most hardships by following the old mule's example. Shake off the dirt, keep looking up, and keep doing the work. If you maintain your commitment and your positive attitude, you'll eventually climb out of your trial. Sometimes, all success requires is the right perspective.

Athlete Huddle

How do you handle adversity? Are you more like the farmer or the mule?

Coach Huddle

What is one of the hardest challenges you've ever faced? How has it impacted the way you coach?

134

The Paradox of Competition

Henk Kraaijenhof

International Performance Consultant - HelpingTheBestToGetBetter.com

Elite sport is simple in its outcome: you either win or you lose. And maybe that is part of what makes it so beautiful. After running a personal best and winning an Olympic silver medal, one of my athletes asked me, "So what is going to happen now?"

I told her, "This is the paradox of winning. Everything changes and nothing changes at the same time. People will recognize you. They will say they always knew you'd make it this far, even if they said the opposite behind your back. You will have many, many friends. Journalists will first ask you about your race, then about track and field, and soon about sports in general. And it won't be long before they ask you questions about politics, science or economy. This race will change your life.

"At the same time, nothing will change. You'll still have to sleep and eat, and worst of all, tomorrow you'll be at the track at ten o'clock, and so will I. Keep in mind that one day your record will be broken and your medal will be in a drawer or on a wall. But it's a symbol, a priceless gift you've given yourself. What will remain is the memory of us working together, our fun and our stress, our smarts and our stupidity. You'll always have that. Cherish it."

Athlete Huddle

What kind of example do you want to set for your fans? If you could send one message with your life, what would it be?

Coach Huddle

If success in sport is momentary, then what is your true goal? What will you spend your career building?

135

Playing Favorites

Matt Krause

Director of Strength & Conditioning - New York Yankees

W hat follows is a story I encountered a while back by the great basketball coach John Leonard. I can't even remember where I found it, but I've used it ever since. It's now presented front and center in our manuals and on our website.

These days, there's a lot of talk about treating people fairly. As a coach, that insinuates I should give equal attention to all of my athletes. But I don't. Like Leonard, I can only offer my time and attention. And I choose to focus most of that energy on those who show up with a good attitude, ready to listen, ready to ask questions, ready to give maximum effort.

John Leonard:

One day a few years ago, a club board member accused me of "having favorites" on our team. Several other parent board members nodded their heads in agreement. The implication was that this was a terrible sin. When I was a younger coach, I thought it was terrible also. And he was right. I did have favorites. My favorites were those athletes who most fervently did what I asked of them. Those that did, I gave more attention to. I talked to them more. I spent more time teaching them. I also expected more of them.

The implication that he was making was that my favorites got better than the others because they were my favorites, and that was somehow unfair. He mistook cause for effect.

The fact is that the athletes who came to me ready to learn, ready to listen, ready to act on what they learned, and try it my way, even if it was more challenging, more difficult than they imagined, were ready to get more out of our program. And they were my favorites.

As a coach, I have only one thing to offer athletes. That is my attention. Which means that I attend to their needs. The reward for good behavior should be attention. The consequence of inattention, lack of effort, unwillingness or lack of readiness to learn, or just plain offensive or disruptive behavior is my inattention to that athlete.

How could it be other than this? If you have three children, and you spend all of your time and energy working with the one that behaves badly, what does that tell your other two children? It tells them that to capture your attention, they must behave badly. What we reward is what we get. As a coach, I want athletes who are eager to learn, eager to experiment, and eager to work hard. I want athletes who come to me for help in developing their skills, both mental and physical, athletes who are willing to accept what I have to offer. Otherwise, why have they come to me? And I am going to reward that athlete with my attention. In so doing, I encourage others to become like the athlete reward. If I spent my time with the unwilling, the slothful, the disruptive, I would only be encouraging that behavior.

The link I want to forge is between attention and excellence. Excellence in the sense of achieving all that is possible and desired. My way of forging that is to offer my attention to those who "attend to me." This of course results in increased performance for those that do so. I am a coach, and when I pay attention to a person, that person is going to improve. Over time, this makes it appear that my "favorites" are the better players, but that

286

isn't quite accurate. The better players are those that pay attention and thus become my favorites. The coach's job is to reward those who exhibit positive developmental behavior. These are my "favorites," and they should be!

Athlete Huddle

Do you show up on time? Do you ask questions to get better? Are you giving your best effort? Do you behave like a favorite?

Coach Huddle

Have you defined your standard? Do your athletes know what it takes to become one of your favorites?

136

Being a Champion

Matt Balis

Director of Football Performance - Notre Dame

B eing a champion is an all-the-time thing. That means you are a champion when you train, practice, go to class, and when you're with your friends. Most days, being the best is hard and requires you to make tough decisions. It requires a great attitude, focus, attention to detail, and grit. These decisions are moment by moment. You make them when you wake up in the morning, go to class, deal with your classmates and teachers. You make them when you prepare to practice or weight train, when deciding how to attack a practice or weight training session, deciding what your mindset will be.

However, some of the hardest decisions you will make will be when you are with your friends, when you have to recover and take care of yourself by eating and hydrating. The sacrifices you make in order to ensure you are getting better each day for yourself and the team will determine our success in the coming season.

You guys have to be a family and surround yourselves with our brotherhood: guys you can trust that have your best interest in mind. There is no decision more important than who you choose to hang out with when you are away from the facility. How you choose to spend your time and who you choose to spend it with will determine your future, and ultimately ours as a program. What you see, hear and feel each day is having a much more profound effect on you than you may realize. We need everyone on this team making right decisions that affect our team in a positive way.

This doesn't mean you need to be perfect. Being perfect is not the goal. Excellence is the goal: trying to be the best you can be by adopting the mindset of a champion each and every day.

Athlete Huddle

What does it mean to you to be a champion? How to champions behave? What decisions to champions make?

Coach Huddle

How important is trust in the development of a successful team? How can you stimulate the growth of trust in a group of young people?

137

Purpose and Passion

Gus Felder

Strength Coach - Georgia Tech University

The Bible tells the story of how God is both present and involved in every aspect of our lives. When you open that book, one person who really stands out is Paul. Paul's a guy who's clearly passionate about his calling. He figures out what he stands for, what his purpose is, and then he pursues it with vigor.

I love highlighting the life of Paul because it provides a great example of how we should respond to life's pressures. We may not find ourselves imprisoned. We may not find ourselves shipwrecked. But we can surely learn from a man who didn't allow the world's noise to distract him from his calling.

Similar to Paul, we live with a culture that easily distracts. And staying focused is especially hard for student-athletes. There are the long, busy days, the classwork and assignments, the grueling practices. There's pressure from family and friends at home. There's social media. There are early morning workouts. There's almost no downtime.

I've found that most students athletes struggle so badly because they don't take time to wrestle with life's big questions. What drives you to do all this? What is God's purpose for you? What's his plan for your life? Many people call this you're "why." But I've found that your "why" turns into your "how" if you don't find your purpose and pursue it with passion.

Before his dramatic conversion, Paul's passion was misplaced. His purpose was totally different. As a Pharisee, he'd garnered respect. He could have boasted about his accomplishments, about his social rank. Yet Paul said that he considered all of that to be garbage when compared with the value of knowing Jesus.

After his conversion, Paul discovered a new purpose and unquenchable passion. That purpose shaped the rest of his life. That purpose is still making ripples today.

Athlete Huddle

What's your purpose? What's your passion? What's the one thing that you stand for above all else?

Coach Huddle

How often do you consider the human beings your coaching, not just the athletes? What impact are you making beyond the weight room?

138

The Power of Struggle

Lachlan Wilmot

Head of Athletic Performance/Co-Owner - Parramatta Eels NRL Club/Athletes Authority

There's a common story of a man who discovers the chrysalis of a developing butterfly. Fascinated, he watches as the miraculous creature works to break through its cocoon and free itself. Hours pass. The butterfly's strength seems to wane, and still the shell remains intact. This is a moment we all recognize, isn't it? Like the butterfly, we've all faced circumstances that seem impossible to surmount.

After a brief rest, the butterfly continues its work and manages to poke a hole in the shell. But as it fights to force itself through, it gets stuck. It doesn't move. For several moments, the man watches. Then he thinks, this creature has fought hard enough. Surely I can help it the rest of the way. So he reaches out and breaks off a piece of the cocoon.

At first, the butterfly doesn't seem to notice. But after a few seconds, it emerges slowly, its brand new wings shriveled, its exhausted body swollen. The man waits for the insect to stretch its wings and take flight, to realize the miracle of metamorphosis. But as we who've heard the story know, it never does. Why?

Forcing the butterfly to fight through its own cocoon is nature's way of strengthening the creature's wings for flight. Without the struggle, there's no victory. There's no miracle.

Here's the point. Our struggles aren't mere obstacles we face on the road to success. They pave the way. Without our struggles, we never grow. We never get stronger. We never realize the miracles we were made to achieve. So tackle your hardships head on. Don't rely on help from others. Claim your struggle. Claim your victory.

Athlete Huddle

What events in your life have molded you? How do you use the struggles you've faced to make yourself better?

Coach Huddle

What struggles have you faced? How could they help you reach your athletes? Do you think they make you a better coach?

139

Cypress Dome

John Garrish

Director of Athletic Development - North Broward Preparatory School (FL)

A cypress dome is a unique kind of swamp. It's made of cypress trees that form what appears to be a forest on a hill. The trees central to the swamp are progressively taller than those on the outside, so if you were just driving by, you'd probably assume that all of the trees were the same height, that the dome appearance was caused by a hill beneath. But the opposite is true. The higher canopy trees are taller. And stronger. The ground beneath them is not a hill; it's a depression that, at its greatest depth, offers deeper water and more fertile soil: better growing conditions.

We're like trees in a cypress dome. Living on the outside is safe, comfortable and common. The greater the perimeter of the swamp, or the greater the number of people in a social circle, the more people

live along the outside, easily blending in but never experiencing significant growth. The trees central to the swamp have greater depth. They've started their journeys at a lower point. They've been flooded and buried, trashed and stepped on. They've experienced apparent disadvantages. But in the end, their depth has afforded conditions for exemplary growth and unmistakable success.

Sometimes we don't understand why we feel pain, why we lose or why we hit rock bottom. But those are the moments that teach us how to prevail, overcome and use what once plagued us to flourish.

Athlete Huddle

What's the greatest loss you ever experienced in sport? How did you bounce back? What did you learn?

Coach Huddle

What was your rock bottom? What about your greatest success? Is there any correlation between the two?

140

Stumbling Baby

Nick Grantham

Performance Enhancement Specialist - NickGrantham.com

How do you get good at something? By learning from your mistakes, right? I guarantee you that no successful athlete ever achieve the top of his or her sport on talent alone. Success requires work. At one point, every skilled athlete was a stumbling baby.

Think about it. How do babies learn to walk? Do they just roll over one day, get up and start strutting around? No, they work hard. For months, they barely move. As they grow, they learn to roll. They learn to crawl. Most of all, they learn to fail. They learn to hold themselves up. They're wobbly at first. They fall a lot. None of this is easy, and all this time, they've not even attempted walking.

Babies know that in order to walk they have to keep trying. They have to fall over. They stumble, wobble, bump into things and start over. But with every slip, trip and fall they learn. They hone their skills, they refine their strategies. They plan for another attempt. Babies are really comfortable with failing. They are happy to keep on trying until they nail it.

The training process is never straightforward. Learning a new lift, running a new play, striving for a faster time: it all takes time. You'll encounter setbacks. You will stumble and fall. The main thing is to learn as you go. Embrace the process. Be patient. Be consistent. Persevere.

Athlete Huddle

Can you relate to the stumbling baby? Are you comfortable with failure? Are you prepared to be bad at something before you can be good at it?

Coach Huddle

Do you fail enough? Do you stretch yourself enough? Are you willing to be imperfect? Do you model the kind of vulnerability and perseverance you want to see in your athletes?

141

Not Good Enough for Frustration

Dan John

Coach & Author - DanJohn.net

One of the toughest issues we deal with in the weight room is frustration. My old boss once said: "The most spoiled generation in history had kids. Good luck." I've had frustrated parents tell me how hard their kids have worked. But usually, they're wrong.

Sure, these kids have the energy drinks and the expensive gear. They know how to taunt their opponents and beat their chests, but they don't understand the hard work that success requires.

Parents saying their kids are frustrated: of course, that reminds me of a story.

Gary Player was one of the most successful golfers in history. One day, a round got the best of him. As he stormed off the course, a fan yelled at him, "I'd give anything for one of your bad days!" As the story goes, Player paused, looked at the fan and retorted, "No, you wouldn't."

He later said that he hears those remarks all the time. But he'd never seen those fans out at the driving range, practicing as the sun rose. Those fans had never swung so many times their hands bled into their gloves. They wouldn't give anything. They wouldn't even give a lot. They didn't understand that they weren't good enough to be frustrated.

You're not good enough to be frustrated.

If you spend seventeen years mastering your craft, you're allowed to feel frustrated. If you've only spent seventeen minutes, pipe down and keep practicing.

Showing up for a training session with the rest of the team is okay. Showing up early is better. Finding time in the offseason to master fundamentals is far better. If I see you struggling to master a movement, I'll help you try a different approach. If that doesn't work, we'll keep trying new methods until we run out of time and energy. And then we'll get up and keep trying.

We're not going to invite frustration into these sessions. I just don't think you're good enough.

Athlete Huddle

Have you ever felt like quitting because you couldn't master something? Did you keep going?

Coach Huddle

At what point do you become good enough to feel frustrated?

142

The Most Important Decision of the Day

Bo Sandoval

Director of Strength & Conditioning - UFC Performance Institute

The most important decision of the day confronts you the moment you open your eyes. Are you going to attack the day, or are you going to hit the snooze button? That moment is frequently challenging, but it also offers you the opportunity to set your tone for the day. In that moment, you dictate the level of productivity at which you'll be operating for the next twelve hours.

Now, some factors are beyond your control. Some days are bad. We all have those. Sometimes mistakes have already been made, and there's nothing to do except press on. But we still have the chance to dig in with a persevering mindset, regardless of our circumstances. And that starts the moment we wake up.

Some days, this is an easy decision. On game day, everyone's jacked up on confidence and ready to impose the team's united will. Other days, it doesn't come as freely. Those are the situations in which we dictate the feeling. We command it. We decide to rise up and claim that positive mindset, even though it's not naturally present. Those are the days that really matter. Learn to control your attitude. Learn to be consistent. Learn to attack each day the same, whether it's a game day or not.

The question I often ask myself as I open my eyes is whether I'm going to be an energy giver or an energy taker. Which will it be? Givers always have something to contribute (time, energy, etc.). Takers exhaust those around them by spreading negativity. Make generosity a habit.

Athlete Huddle

Are you giving or taking? Do you get up each day, determined to excel or contented with getting by?

Coach Huddle

How can your body language affect the tone of a training session? What can you do to improve the energy of your team or organization?

143

The Panther, the Vine and the Strawberry

Todd Hamer

Director of Strength & Conditioning - George Washington University

I got this story from Ethan Reeves, and I share it with my athletes at least three times each semester. It evolves with each telling, and while I encourage coaches to make it their own, I have to give credit to Ethan.

As a young man, I grew up in a region full of hills, woods and valleys. One day, while exploring the countryside, I heard an ominous sound behind me and turned to see a crouched panther eyeing me from several yards away. For a second, I was scared motionless. But then I broke into a desperate sprint, the hungry beast hot on my heels.

Moments later, I arrived at the edge of a steep cliff. Behind me the panther growled, preparing to pounce. I had no time. I grabbed a nearby vine that stretched down into the precipice and began to hastily descend. When I got about halfway down, I paused to catch my breath. Up above, the animal watched me. I looked down and saw to my dismay that a second panther awaited me at the bottom. I was trapped! And as I hung there, clinging to that vine, considering my hopeless plight, I saw a small band of mice nibbling at my lifeline just a few feet above me. What was I to do?

That's when I finally noticed a small strawberry bush growing beside me on the cliff face. There was only one berry that I could see, and it wasn't ripe. In fact, it had bird droppings on it. But I plucked all the same and tasted it. It was delicious.

Moments later, the mice finished chewing through the vine and I fell to my death. That's the end of the story. What's the moral? Well, I still see myself as that young man. The first panther represents my past. No matter what I do, it's still there. It's still ready to consume me if I let it. The second panther is my future. Sooner or later, we all reach the end of the story. The mice demonstrate the passage of time. They remind me that the clock never stops ticking, that the vine to which I cling may snap at any moment. The strawberry is everything else. The strawberry is your choice. Some days it may be ripe and full of flavor. Some days it may be covered in droppings. But only you get to decide what you'll do. My advice would be to focus on the strawberry. Focus on the good. Focus on what you can control. That's the way to living a meaningful life.

Athlete Huddle

What choices are you making? What are you choosing to focus on, the strawberry or something else?

Coach Huddle

How much time do you spend considering things that are beyond your control? Do you invest in yourself as much as you do in your athletes?

144

Feeling Burned Out

Lew Caralla

Head Football Strength & Conditioning Coach - Georgia Tech University

Every sports team should have this read to them annually:

"If you guys are really wondering if you are burning out mentally, take a day off and go to your local hospital. Go to the cancer wing. Look at a four-year-old who won't ever see their teenage years, probably won't ever see their next birthday. Go and see someone who is mentally or physically [handicapped], or see when a soldier who just came back from war doesn't have legs anymore. Stare that guy down. Look him right in the eyes and tell him, as you stand there with two capable legs, that you are burned out. That you don't want to use them. See if that doesn't kill him right there. Because he would do anything to have that opportunity." - Greg Plitt.

Every year, there are full scholarship athletes with all the talent and resources to be successful. Yet they still complain about everything. This message normally is extremely impactful and leaves them speechless and thoughtful. What is my excuse? What is really holding me back? It reminds them not to take what they have for granted and challenges them to stop making excuses.

Athlete Huddle

What is stopping you?

Coach Huddle

List three things you take for granted every day.

145

When the Sun Comes Up

Micah Kurtz

Director of Sports Performance - Windermere Preparatory School (SC)

What did you do when you woke up this morning? Maybe you checked your phone, checked your Instagram likes or checked your Twitter followers. Or maybe some of you woke up thinking about playing video games. I'm not saying that all of these are bad things. Social media can be a great tool for networking and learning. But we only get 24 hours in a day. Time is the most valuable commodity in the world. We are all allotted the same number of seconds each day, and those who spend their time doing things that help them achieve their aspirations are the most successful.

Christopher McDougall once wrote: "Every morning in Africa, a gazelle wakes up and knows it must outrun the fastest lion or be killed. Every morning in Africa, a lion wakes up and it knows it must run faster than the slowest gazelle or starve to death. It doesn't matter whether you're the lion or the gazelle; when the sun comes up, you'd better be running."

Spend your time wisely today and chase your dreams. Make sure you spend your time doing the things that will move you closer to achieving your goals.

Athlete Huddle

How much time do you spend on social media or playing video games? What would happen if you spent some of that time doing something that would push you toward achieving your short-term goals?

Coach Huddle

How could you do a better job of demonstrating to your athletes the importance of putting time to good use?

146

Making a Difference

Donnie Maib

Head Coach Athletic Performance - University of Texas at Austin

Every summer, an author would live at the beach to focus on his writing and get away from distractions. One early morning, as he looked out of his window, he saw a young man who appeared to be dancing down by the water's edge. Puzzled, the author went outside and walked toward the water to investigate. As he got closer, he noticed that the youth wasn't dancing at all. He was picking up starfish and throwing them back into the ocean. The sand was covered with thousands of the creatures.

"What are you doing?" the author asked, as he finally came up to the boy.

"I'm throwing these starfish back into the ocean." The author looked around. The starfish seemed to go on forever.

"You're wasting your time," he said. "You'll never make a difference."

The young man laughed as picked up another starfish and hurled it into the surf. "I just made a difference for that one!"

The difference between success and failure is sometimes as simple as perspective. If we're diligent and joyful in our work, the small differences we make will multiply over time. It starts with just one.

Athlete Huddle

Do you want to be a difference maker? What are some ways you can impact your team today?

Coach Huddle

Do you relate more to the author or the young man?

147

Three Keys to Success That Require No Talent

Jim Kielbaso

President - International
Youth Conditioning Association

Whenever I see that a group needs to consider some basic success principles, I start out at the ground level and teach them three keys to success (and these apply to all aspects of life) that require no talent. All three build on each other, and they're once explained, it's easy to revisit them during practice or competition.

1. Show Up. Show up on time, where you're supposed to be, prepared to give your best effort. That means having the right shoes, clothes and equipment, and taking the necessary steps to optimize your physical and mental readiness. This requires no talent, but not doing it can cause a tremendously negative consequence.

2. Listen to directions and follow them to the best of your ability. Too often, teams break down because someone neglects to listen or fails to cooperate. Listening and following directions are skills that require practice, but no team has ever achieved massive success without them. When you hear a coach begin to speak, practice attentiveness. When directions are given, practice following them. It can mean all difference in crunch time,

when a game's on the line. Have you ever witnessed a play in which one player failed to perform his or her assignment? If so, you know how that ends. Be the best at listening and following instructions.

3. Give one hundred percent. Commit to what you're doing and give your best effort. It often feels safer to hold back a little, because if you fail, you can tell yourself you weren't trying your hardest. But holding back never leads to praiseworthy outcomes. Be the kind of person who gives exceptional effort, and you will achieve exceptional results.

Many people live with regrets. Giving max effort not only produces great results. It also limits regrets. Again, none of these keys require any talent, but they have the potential to create massive success in all areas of life. While they may seem too simple to matter, not following them will greatly diminish your chance of success. And following them consistently enhances your reputation and positions you to accomplish great things.

Athlete Huddle

Do you ever think about how hard you're competing? Does your effort depend on the situation? What would happen if you gave your all right out of the gate?

Coach Huddle

How can you demonstrate for your athletes the value of approaching sport with the mindset of limiting regrets?

148

Culture

Mike Bewley

Director of Basketball Strength & Conditioning - Clemson University

For teams, culture is something that can't be overlooked. Building a culture you and your team can be proud of takes time and energy. If you're not willing to put in the work developing that culture, chances of the team being successful are slim.

Have you ever been on a team that was invaded with negativity, poor leadership and conflict? It can be very frustrating since, no matter how hard the athletes train, poor team culture seems to continuously interfere with the team consistently performing their best. As a strength and conditioning coach, you have a unique opportunity to assist the head sport coach in building the team culture they envision. By getting on the same page, you can have a big impact on how the team gets along, functions, and ultimately performs.

A team's culture is the expression of the team's attitudes, characteristics and beliefs. Therefore, the culture creates norms of acceptable behavior on a team. Such standards usually dictate how the team acts, communicates, assists, and deals with conflict. When clear rules are established, everyone on a team is more likely to abide by them.

Most importantly, the culture creates an atmosphere that permeates every aspect of a team's experience. Is the atmosphere laid back or intense? Care-free or competitive? Encouraging or disparaging?

All of these qualities of culture have impactful implications for how the team functions, how teammates get along, and how each player performs. When a team has a defined culture that is understood and can be recited by all of its members, they feel a sense of belonging and have a sincere willingness to support that culture.

Athlete & Coach Huddle

As a strength and conditioning coach, don't limit your role exclusively to training. Take the time to sit down with the entire coaching staff, as well as your athletes, to discuss the kind of culture the team wants to have. Here are some questions to ponder together:

1. What values do we want to act as the foundation for our team culture?

2. Can the players, position coaches and ancillary staff (managers, grad assistants, etc.) recall and define the team's foundational principles?

3. Do players know their strengths and weaknesses?

4. Do players know how much time they should devote to enhancing their strength and what they need to work on in the weight room?

5. What attitudes do you want to have and what beliefs do you want to hold about your sport, competition, and team?

6. What are the goals that the team wants to pursue?

7. How do the athletes and coaches want to treat each other?

8. What kind of atmosphere do we want on this team?

9. After I (the strength coach) build the team's culture in the offseason, how will the coaching staff continue to support the culture during the competitive season?

149

Two Sides of Culture

Jay DeMayo

Head Strength Coach Basketball - University of Richmond

Side One: Heads, the Coaching Staff

I've spoken about this a few times and even written an entire series on my webpage about what a single meeting I was in led to. In a 2-hour discussion, we saved a relationship and changed the entire direction of a program.

We all have "that team" with "that coach." A really nice person that you just don't mesh with. For some reason, it always seems to be some petty garbage, too. With this staff, it was simply the words we were speaking to each other. In this amazing world of instant information, people seem to have found a vast array of definitions for simple terms. So many in fact that people truly can mean ten different things when using vocabulary in daily discussions. The word of the day for this meeting was "fit."

I can imagine coaches' eyes rolling right now. That word is up there with "core" for me when it comes to coaches using it and having no idea what they are trying to say. I had finally had enough. I stood up at the meeting, erased the board and said, "What does fit mean to you?"

Asking that question stopped the room and led to more questions. Those questions drove an actual discussion about the people who are most

315

important: the student-athletes. This led to how we planned on evaluating the team, which led to how we planned to prepare the team. We broke down every test: why we thought it would be important and how it would help the team. We then looked at the actual training and deciphered if it would set them up to be successful in both the tests we were asking them to perform.

For the first time, I walked out of a meeting with that staff, feeling that there was actual potential. I now had a group that was completely in my corner and truly understood what we were trying to do. To be honest, it saved a working relationship with a great staff and an awesome team.

Side Two: Tails, the Players

This same team is made up of some of the most fantastic young women I've ever worked with. They train their butts off. But for a few weeks, I started to take a hard look and asked myself, "Are they really bought in or just compliant?" So I did the one thing I think we should do more of: I asked the players. At first, they were taken aback by someone asking their opinion of what their preparation should be, but they quickly opened up.

We sat down and they told me they felt the team was really strong, but that they needed to be in way better shape than they were. I asked them to elaborate and they did. They broke it all down. They told me what parts they thought were really working, where they saw weaknesses and gave reasons why. All I did was listen and write down what they said. When they finished, I thanked them and told them how grateful I was for their input, that I was meeting with the coaches (see above) that afternoon.

Once the plan was laid out with the coaches, I went back to the four athletes I talked with before to review it with them. They immediately bought in. What was this amazing change we made to the program, you ask? Instead of lifting three times a week and running two, we switched to running three times a week and lifting two. That change, that drastic amount

316

of autonomy, had their investment rate at an all-time high. They were pushing each other every day. "This is what we wanted. Now let's go!"

This continued throughout the summer leading up to camp. When the team returned, we ran our conditioning tests and there is one that's a bear. The team is so petrified of it that's it's more of a mind game than a physical evaluation. The largest group to finish it in our tenure here was five, but this year we had 12. To be completely frank with you, I think three more should have passed but that's another talk for another day.

The team's culture shifted the minute I quit trying to push square pegs into round holes and started listening to my team. You want to change a culture? Then listen to both sides' input: the coaches and the players. Lead them to success, see their sense of pride grow, and make sure they know you have their back no matter what.

Athlete Huddle

Are you being honest with yourself and your coach about the strength of your current program? What would you change to make it better?

Coach Huddle

Are you breaking down your program with your staff so everyone is on the same page? Are you asking for the player's input?

150

The Boulder and the King

Adam Feit

Coordinator of Physical and Mental Performance - Springfield College

Many years ago, there was a curious king. During a time of social unrest, he sought to test the determination of his people. So he placed a huge boulder in the middle of a main road that led through the city. He then hid nearby to see what would happen. Would anyone try to remove the obstruction?

The first people to pass by were some of the king's wealthiest merchants and lords. Instead of trying to move the boulder, they simply scoffed and walked around it. A few of them even blamed the King for not maintaining better roads. Not one of them tried to address the problem.

Hours later, after many had passed by, a lowly peasant came along, his arms full of firewood. When he saw the boulder, he put down his load and did his best to push it off the road. At last, he succeeded. And as the boulder rolled away, it revealed a purse lying beneath it.

Bewildered, the peasant picked up the purse and discovered numerous gold coins inside, along with a note from the king. The note said the coins were a reward from the crown for moving the boulder.

What's the moral of the story? When it comes to adversity, we have power. We're able in many cases to change our circumstances. Ryan

Holiday, author of The Obstacle is the Way, reminds us that "The obstacle in the path becomes the path. Never forget, within every obstacle is an opportunity to improve our condition." If we sit around and argue, complain or give up, we're accepting our fate for what it is. We're not doing anything to change course. We're stifling our future. So rather than whine about our misfortunes and mistakes, why not review what happened and rise above? Are you going to be a part of the problem or a part of the solution?

Athlete Huddle

What's holding you back from reaching greatness? Could changing your course get you closer to the finish line?

Coach Huddle

What are some of the obstacles in your path? What would happen if you started viewing challenges as opportunities for growth?

151

Ladder and Harvest

Fred Eaves

Director of Athletics and Wellness - Battle Ground Academy

At Battle Ground Academy, we live by two laws in our athletics program: the law of the ladder and the law of the harvest. The law of the ladder is our way of describing a step-by-step process. We believe strongly that the right process equals the right outcome. The law of the harvest is a term we use to emphasize that hard work equals success. We want our athletes to understand that you reap what you sow.

We use a specific story from early in my tenure at BGA with one of our best football teams to drive these concepts home. This was probably the most mature, hard-working and resilient team I have had the opportunity to coach in my 20 years in the field. The group was driven by a stellar senior class that embodied our core values of hard work, enthusiasm, accountability, resilience, and teamwork - or heart, as we refer to it at The Academy.

As great as this group of young men became their senior year, they were the exact opposite the previous season. They were selfish, entitled, and consistently placing blame on each other in a very disappointing junior campaign at our school. We were a preseason pick to play for a state championship and we ended up being upset in the last seconds to a team we should have handled with ease. The entire year, we looked past opponents to a matchup with the no. 1 ranked team in the state, and we did not display consistent work ethic to match our goals for the season.

It was a week-to-week battle to keep this group focused on the task at hand. Despite all of this, we won our district and entered the playoffs as a no. 1 seed in our bracket. We had a good draw in the playoffs and looked poised to make a run at the championship game if we handeld our business each week.

The week of the quarterfinal game was an extremely cold week in middle Tennessee. We were practicing in low 20s temperatures to prepare for the game that was going to be in the teens. All week our kids were focused on the poor weather and really had no sense of urgency regarding the matchup. We continued to work to get them dialed in with little to no success that week. It was one of the most frustrating weeks of practice I have ever been associated with.

We struggled in the contest from the outset and ended up turning the ball over six times on our way to giving up a touchdown one yard with 30 seconds left in the game to lose 21-17. When the horn blew, we had players laying on the ground crying. The game had been a complete disaster.

I looked around and saw our unquestioned leader laying on the ground crying with the rest of the group. He was our leader, but unfortunately, he never led in the right direction. He had been our biggest distraction that year. I walked up to him and asked him to get up off the ground. He gave me a strange look and I explained to him he had no reason to lay on the ground and cry. The young man slowly started to stand up, but he still had no idea why I was telling him to get up.

I looked him directly in the eye and referred to our two laws. I asked him if he believed we had followed these two laws throughout this season and especially this week. We overlooked this opponent which broke the law of the ladder and we did not work very hard to prepare for this opponent, which broke the law of the harvest. It seemed very simple to me, but it hadn't seemed to resonate with him until this moment. I proceeded to explain to him that we would never reach our potential in his time with our program until he bought in, and I challenged him to lead our team in the direction it should be going instead of straight down the toilet. I told him, "You have to earn the right to lay on the ground through your actions each day. Your actions dictate who you really are. Remember, the right process equals the right outcome."

He slowly but surely turned into the young man we were looking for by next season. When we lined up the next year, we were a different group with essentially the same team returning. We were a group that followed the laws to a tee, and it was evident every Friday night. We progressed every week and after a dominant performance in the semifinals, we earned the right to play for a state championship. We battled and ultimately came up short to a great team that was the better team that night. This young man took the loss extremely hard and we sat in the quad the next day discussing his journey over the past year and how different he was as a person.

He made a comment that allowed me to refer back to our conversation on the field at the end of the previous year. He said, "Coach, we just didn't leave our mark on the program. We didn't win the state championship." I asked him if he remembered what we discussed on the field that night last fall and he said he did.

I responded, "You should lay your head down and sleep well. You and your classmates did everything the right way. You worked hard and consistently improved each week of the season. You gave your very best effort every time you stepped on a practice field or a game field, and I promise you that you and your classmates have left your mark on this program. It hurts today and it will hurt 20 years from now, but you have earned the right to hurt and you have earned the right to be proud of everything you have accomplished. I have never coached an athlete or a

322

team that has had as dramatic a turnaround as you and this team have, and I will never forget it. This team will always be one of my favorites, if not my favorite team. You don't need a ring for that."

I share this with our kids because this story explains why we do what we do each day. It helps explain what we believe in at BGA. Many of our current players watched this team in lower or middle school and it is still relevant to them. We help turn boys into men of character by what we do with them each day in the weight room and on the field. As coaches, we have to live by these two laws, as well. As a staff, we gave those kids everything we had and more on and off the field, and it was one of the most enjoyable years I have ever coached. I can undoubtedly say that it was my favorite team I have ever coached.

These young men were true champions, regardless of the final result of that championship game. The young man I discussed earlier became a leader in life as well. He is very successful and he attributes his experience in our program as life-changing for him. In the end, who they become down the road and how they affect our world are all that really matters.

Athlete Huddle

What can you take away from our story at BGA? Do you have the right attitude and the focus every day to meet your end goals? If not, what will you do to change that?

Coach Huddle

What are your laws? How are you enforcing them daily and getting the team to buy in? Are you following the laws yourself?

152

Failure as Feedback

Nick Winkelman

Head of Athletic Performance & Science - Irish Rugby Football Union

Athletes, do you enjoy failure?

That's an easy question, right? Nobody wants to fail. Nobody enjoys losing. People talk a lot about how defeat is important, how it creates opportunities for growth and improvement. But there's still a stigma attached to the word. We still run from failure. Why? It's because we as competitors aim for perfection. We aim for the top of the podium. Failure comes between us and our goals, right?

Wrong. From now on, let's stop viewing failure as a setback. Failure is feedback. It tells us things about ourselves that we previously didn't realize. And that information is useful. It helps us identify ways to improve our performance, both mentally and physically. It sets us on the path to perfection.

What's the alternative? Running away from mistakes? Playing it safe? That mindset will never take us to our limits, and unless we discover our limits, we'll never learn to push past them. Perfection means we've arrived. It means there's no further room for growth. Let's adopt a growth mentality. Let's embrace failure, understanding that it's nothing more than feedback. And feedback paves the way to our better selves.

Athlete Huddle

How can you apply the concept of failure as feedback in the weight room? How might your training look different if you sought out failure instead of avoiding it?

Coach Huddle

How can you set a good example for your athletes of embracing failure as a means to growth?

153

Positive Attitude: Don't Miss a Moment

Gary Schofield

Southeast Director - PLAE

There is a saying that the squeaky wheel gets the grease. It's so easy to point out what is wrong. It is easy to complain about what we don't like. And when we do complain, we often get a response, which reinforces the habit. Similarly, we rarely worry about oil changes or tire pressure until the warning light comes on. Only then do we take the car in to get serviced. The world around us has become inundated with negative news. Turn on the television. What stories get coverage? Fires, thefts, accidents, disasters, etc.

One late Sunday afternoon, I was watching The Last Samurai, and a statement made by Katsumoto (a Japanese warrior seeking to explain his people's lifestyle to a foreigner) hit me like a ton of bricks. Katsumoto says, "I come to this place of my ancestors, and I remember. Like these blossoms, we are all dying. To know life in every breath, every cup of tea, every life we take. The way of the warrior...that is Bushido." I couldn't shake the truth of that sentiment. Life is short. Why do we spend so much time obsessing over the negatives instead of celebrating the positives? Choosing to live means choosing to feel life in each breath. It's what we're born to do.

Athlete Huddle

How do you respond when a teammate demonstrates a negative attitude? Do you ever set aside time to practice mindfulness and gratitude?

Coach Huddle

It's our job to evaluate the strengths and weakness of our athletes. Which do you spend more time focusing on? Is your approach as effective as it could be?

154

The Wood Pile

Mickey Marotti

Assistant Athletic Director/FB Sports Performance - Ohio State University

Every training cycle, every offseason program, every summer program starts with the same conversation. We have a real, honest, passionate meeting about objectives. We talk about the plan, what it involves, what our athletes will get out of it, and what our expectations of them are. What's the standard? We define it and we enforce it. Falling short is unacceptable.

Players, understand that it's bigger than you. It's about the players of the past, present and the future. It's about this university and what it stands for. It's about the guy next to you. It's about brotherhood. It's about us.

We believe in what we call the power of the unit. In your group, hold each other accountable. It's up to you to build your culture. Fight for each other, train for each other, and sweat for each other. G. K. Chesterton said, "The true soldier fights not because he hates what is in front of him, but because he loves what is behind him." Work for your brothers.

I talk a lot about hard work, old-school, dirty, sweaty work. There's a story of a dad who tells his little boy to chop some wood. When the boy's done, he's instructed to stack it all. What a sense of accomplishment!

There's joy to be found in doing a job well, in not taking shortcuts. Just when the boy thinks he's done, his dad tells him to move the wood pile to the other side of the barn. This story is important because it illustrates the value of grit. In our modern world, we have so much information at our fingertips. A lot of what used to be difficult is now easy. But let's not forget that any success worth achieving requires work ethic.

If you want to succeed in the weight room, you'll work for it. You'll learn to appreciate the grind. There are no shortcuts here, only passion and will.

Athlete Huddle

What drives you? Where do you get your passion from?

Coach Huddle

Who's the hardest worker you've ever known?

155

The Lens

Bryan Mann

Assistant Professor of Kinesiology and Sport Sciences - University of Miami

W hat is your lens? It's your perspective of the world. It's how you interpret what you see. They say history can never truly be recorded, because every perspective is different. The story of one battle, for example, can easily be told in very different ways.

In his book 7 Habits of Highly Effective People, Stephen Covey tells the story of a time he was riding the subway. A man gets on the train with two small children. The children are causing a ruckus, but the man doesn't seem to notice. Stephen thinks to himself, What kind of parent is this guy? He's just allowing his children to annoy other passengers. Eventually, Stephen gets so frustrated that he addresses the man, asking that he control his children. The stranger looks at him blankly, then replies. "Oh, sorry. We just left the hospital. They lost their mother today. They don't know how to handle it. Neither do I." In that moment, Stephen's perspective changes. It goes from one of ignorance and disdain to one of pity and remorse. Did any of the facts actually change? No, just Stephen's lens.

Information frequently changes our perspectives. How does that happen in sport? I asked a few people to answer that question. Here are two of their responses.

Response from an athlete:

When the coach decides to bench you or give someone else your starting position. You want to say it's something personal and he has something against you. I've wanted to say that when it's happened to me. But I've decided that I have to look at it a different way. It's not personal. He has to get paid, too. If he's benching me because he thinks someone else can do better, then it's my job to prove him wrong. He's not seeing it in me because I'm not showing it.

Problems and challenges are separated only by how you view them. Choose to view difficult situations as challenges, chances to improve yourself. There's less stress in that and more positivity.

Response from a staff intern:

Taking things personally isn't the best route to take. It causes a negative experience and tends to result in downward spirals. If you're told something is wrong or isn't good enough, try again and try something different. When you get down to it, it's about your own development. Are you satisfied with where you are? Are you okay with not getting paid? If they tell you that you're not up to snuff, realize that your standards may not be where they should be. You can either get upset about it, or you can grow.

Athlete Huddle

Which lenses are you choosing to look through?

Coach Huddle

Is there ever a time when withholding information from your athletes can help them succeed long-term?

156

Flipping the Switch

Ron Mckeefery

Vice President of Performance & Education - PLAE

I'm not sure there's anything tougher than entering a ring or stepping onto a mat to combat another man or woman. You're waging war on the inside, preparing yourself mentally to battle another human being. And you're managing external stimuli as well, like the lights, the crowds, the fans, etc. In that moment, you have to make all peripheral noise and distraction melt away. You have to flip a switch. I love that moment.

Seeing the greats like Muhammad Ali, Sugar Ray Robinson and Mike Tyson walk to the ring has always fascinated me. You can see the moment written on their faces. Outside of competition, these guys are laid back and pleasant; they have to be. You don't reach that level of fame and success in your sport without learning how to interact with people. And if they unleashed their famous rage and intensity outside the ring, they'd most likely wind up in jail. But as they walk from the dressing room to the ring, they transform their minds into those of trained killers. All of their adrenaline awakens their senses. Their fists become lethal weapons. They prepare to perform.

As coaches, we perform as well. We can control the intensity of any given training session with the energy we bring to the floor. What will that energy be? Will your mind be full of the previous game, issues with another

333

coach, maybe a problem at home? You owe it to your athletes to consistently bring it every day. Learn to flip the switch.

Athlete Huddle

How did you prepare your mind to walk from the locker room to the weight room today?

Coach Huddle

Do you take a moment before each training session to mentally prepare yourself? Are you present in each workout?

157

Napoleon and the Duke

Brett Bartholomew

Strength Coach, Author & Founder - Art of Coaching

B oth in reference to the past and present day, the legendary French general and former emperor Napoleon Bonaparte was widely considered to be nearly unparalleled in his military genius...nearly. What emerged as a result of his genius and his success was a tendency to underestimate his opponents while overestimating his own tactical superiority.

This fatal flaw cost Napoleon towards the end of his reign, most notably during the infamous Battle of Waterloo where he was defeated by Sir Arthur Wellesley (better known as "The First Duke of Wellington") and later exiled to the island of St. Helena where we would spend the rest of his days. Wellesley's steady and calculated strategy was the perfect response to Napoleon's more aggressive leadership style which often relied on heroic tactics, resulting in many French lives lost.

Athlete Huddle

Egos swell and emotions run high in the realm of competition. When we succeed, we have to walk the tightrope between confidence and arrogance, both of which are often nothing more than a shield to protect us from momentary uncertainty. Reflect on a time where you let your pride or impatience lead you down a path to defeat that could have easily been avoided. What feelings were responsible for blinding you to this outcome and how do you go about keeping them in check today?

Coach Huddle

Reflect upon a time where you were under administrative or organizational pressure to deliver results or produce certain outcomes. How did your behavior change as a result of this? What moral dilemmas did it create for you?

Acknowledgements

First and foremost, I want to thank God for having his hand on my life from the very beginning. Without his blessings nothing I have done or will do would be possible.

To my wife, Angie, Thanks for your unconditional love and support. Thank God I had the guts to come ask you to Dance. Team McKeefery starts with you.

To my kids Tyler, Ava, and Maya, I promised myself early in my childhood that I would work my tail off to be the best Father I could possibly be for you. From the moment we met, each day I wake up my hope is that I have lived up to that promise. I love you more than you will ever know.

To my Mom, Laura, I would not be half the man I am if not for your incredible sacrifice to fight against all odds. If not for your love, work ethic, and support I would not have had an example to live up to.

To my siblings Kelly, Pat, Ryan, Celie, and James, Thanks for teaching me competitiveness and perseverance. Our life has not always been easy, but together we have overcome. I am always your big brother and love each of you very much.

To my brother Ricky, who is no longer with us, I miss you each and every day. To Dan Craycraft, David Lane, Dave and Karen Richards, and the rest of my extended Church Family, without you I would not know what unconditional love is.

To all the coaches and teammates I have ever had, your impact has made me the man I am today.

To Tony Dungy, Peter Vaas, Jim Leavitt, Derek Dooley, Marvin Lewis, and Chris Creighton, Thank you for giving me the opportunity to impact young men on your staffs. Your mentorship has made me the coach I am today.

To Tim Maxey, Mark Asanovich, Doug Elias, Chip Morton, and the numerous other Strength and Conditioning mentors I have had thank you for teaching me the ropes and to love this profession.

To all the Strength and Conditioning Coaches that I have had the privilege to work with on my staff, it truly has been my privilege to work with you. You have challenged me each day to be the best S&C Coach I can be.

To the players I have had the opportunity to work with; your impact on me has far outweighed my impact on you. Thank you so much for allowing me to be a part of your life.

To Brett Waits and all the team at PLAE, Thank You for allowing me the opportunity to make a global impact, and do it outside the four walls of a weight room.

To Joe and Ashley Baum, thank you for editing this book, and helping all of us S&C Coaches put forth our best work.

To all the coaches that have contributed to Weight Room Wisdom, Thank you for sharing the inspiring stories you have used with your athletes to help make this profession and world better than we found it.

About The Author

Internationally recognized as a leader in the area of sports development, Ron McKeefery has twice been named Collegiate Strength and Conditioning Coach of the Year. First by the Professional Football Strength and Conditioning Society (2008 Under Armour Collegiate Strength and Conditioning Coach of the Year), and next by the National Strength and Conditioning Association (2016 Collegiate Strength and Conditioning Coach of the Year).

In 2013 Coach McKeefery was honored as a Master Strength and Conditioning Coach by the Collegiate Strength and Conditioning Coaches Association (CSCCa). The Master Strength and Conditioning Coach certification is the highest honor that can be achieved as a strength and conditioning coach, representing professionalism, knowledge, experience, expertise and longevity in the field. In 2019, Coach McKeefery received the Registered Strength and Conditioning Coach Emeritus (RSCC*D) distinction from the NSCA.

Prior to becoming the Vice President of Performance and Education for PLAE, Coach McKeefery served as a strength and conditioning coach at both the Professional and Collegiate level. Working with such professional organizations as the: Cincinnati Bengals (NFL), Kansas City Royals (MLB), Tampa Bay Buccaneers (NFL), and the Berlin Thunder (NFL Europe), and collegiate programs such as: Eastern Michigan University, University of Tennessee, and University of South Florida.

He has had the privilege of working with over 80 players that have gone on to play in the National Football League. Composed of 31 NFL Draft Picks, including 1st Round Draft Pick and Pro Bowlers Mike Jenkins & Jason Pierre-Paul, along with Cordarrelle Patterson and Ja'wuan James. He has had numerous All Americans, NFL free-agents, and All Conference Selections.

Coach McKeefery is a sought after industry speaker. He has lectured for the National Strength and Conditioning Association, Collegiate Strength and Conditioning Association, and numerous International and National Associations/Organizations.

Ron is the author of the #1 Amazon International Bestseller CEO Strength Coach, and has been published in the National Strength and Conditioning journal, American Football Monthly, and several other trade publications.

Now, Coach McKeefery is bringing his expertise and knowledge to PLAE, where he has developed the PLAE Perform Division providing credible, engaging educational resources and safe communal science based training programs all around the world.

Ron McKeefery
RonMcKeefery@gmail.com
Instagram: @RMcKeefery

Made in the USA
Lexington, KY
18 April 2019